THE
Archive Photographs
SERIES
SUPERMARINE

Supermarine Southampton Mk.I military flying-boat near its birthplace at Woolston on the shore of the River Itchen at Southampton in 1926, symbolising the distinctive location, business and excellence of this pioneering British maritime aviation company. The Southampton genus was one of the most successful aircraft, in its class and in its time, ever operated by the Royal Air Force. A splendidly-restored wooden hull of one of these early production Southamptons has recently been brought to public display at the Royal Air Force Museum at Hendon, North London.

THE
Archive Photographs
SERIES

SUPERMARINE

Compiled by
Norman Barfield

CHALFORD

The Chalford Publishing Company
St Mary's Mill, Chalford,
Stroud, Gloucestershire, GL6 8NX

ISBN 0 7524 0605 1

Typesetting and origination by
The Chalford Publishing Company
Printed in Great Britain by
Redwood Books, Trowbridge

Cover Illustration
Spitfire fuselage assembly at the Castle Road Works in Salisbury, Wiltshire, one of the sixty-five dispersal units centred on five towns with supporting airfields across the South of England following the disasterous bombing of the original Vickers-Supermarine factories at Woolston and Itchen, Southampton. Complemented by the huge Government-owned shadow factory at Castle Bromwich, near Birmingham, with its own satellites, this incredibly complex but highly successful wartime production operation realised a grand total of 22,749 Spitfires and Seafires. Most commendably, forty-five per cent of the workforce were women. Significantly, the Spitfire was the only Allied aircraft type in continuous production throughout the Second World War and can thus fairly be regarded as the world's most successful aircraft programme ever.

Contents

The Vickers Aviation Siblings

Popularly known by its distinctive sobriquet 'Supermarine' for virtually the whole of its fifty-year life, from 1913 to 1963, this highly accomplished little aircraft company was, in fact, taken over by Vickers in 1928 and thereafter officially known as Vickers (Aviation) Ltd. Supermarine Works.

Although it continued to operate with almost total autonomy below board level, in parallel with the Vickers main aviation establishment at Weybridge in Surrey (the subject of a separate volume in *The Archive Photographs Series*), in 1938 both the Supermarine Aviation Works (Vickers) Ltd. and its parent company Vickers (Aviation) Ltd. at Weybridge, were taken over by Vickers-Armstrongs Limited.

By the early 1960s the aircraft elements of Supermarine had finally been absorbed into what had by then become Vickers-Armstrongs (Aircraft) Ltd. at Weybridge, until it, too, became one of the three partners in British Aircraft Corporation (BAC) on its formation in 1960. The Vickers name then ultimately disappeared from the British aviation scene altogether with the consolidation of the BAC organisation in 1964 (although Vickers Ltd. continued as a fifty per cent shareholder in BAC). Meanwhile, Supermarine's pioneering Hovercraft work was merged into Saunders-Roe on the Isle of Wight and the Company's non-aircraft business elements were absorbed into Vickers (Engineers) at South Marston, near Swindon.

With the nationalisation of the UK aircraft industry in 1977, BAC became part of the (later privatised) British Aerospace PLC. Although Vickers PLC continues to produce an important range of aerospace products, its main business today lies in the automotive, defence systems, propulsion technology and medical equipment fields. Nevertheless, both Vickers and British Aerospace continue to be proud to count Supermarine among their original illustrious predecessors.

One consequence of the Vickers takeover of Supermarine in November 1928 that is relevant to this book was that all subsequent Supermarine aircraft type numbers were incorporated in the Vickers drawing numbering system at Weybridge. After various numbers between 178 and 240, two blocks – 300 to 399 and 500 to 599 – were allocated to the Supermarine design team. This was the apex of the cascading drawing numbering system, from the complete aircraft general arrangement through to detail parts, that was originally devised by Paul Wyand, the Weybridge Chief Draughtsman, in conjunction with the Air Ministry, in 1919. This system continues to be the the the basis of the nationwide system operated through the Society of British Aerospace Companies (SBAC) today. In practice, however, most types in the Supermarine lineage were generally better known by name and, because of the sibilant, virtually all began with 'S'.

The third component of the Vickers aviation interests was part of Canadian Vickers which was originally established in Montreal as a general engineering and shipbuilding enterprise in 1911 and formed an aviation division in 1922. This company was active in building Vickers types emanating from both Weybridge and Supermarine, those of its own conception and large numbers of many types under licence from other British, Dutch and American aircraft companies, notably during the Second World War. In 1941 Canadian Vickers transferred its aircraft activities to a Government factory at Cartierville before the aircraft division was transferred to the Crown company Canadair Ltd. in 1944, which later became a subsidiary of the American General Dynamics Corporation.

Introduction

The manifestation of the term 'aeronautical' – the science, art and practice of aerial navigation – has always borrowed heavily from the age-old ways and means of the sea. No other aircraft company anywhere in the world better exemplified this conjoinment, or indeed the etymological context of the term itself, in both peace and war, than the aptly-named Supermarine wherein this conjoinment endured as a central theme through the whole of the fifty-year lifetime, from 1913 to 1963, of this small, yet illustrious, British aircraft company.

Its establishment at Southampton, best known as one of the world's most famous seaways serving the 'Port of Ocean Queens', was a natural locale for realising the transition from the marine to the aerial domain during the pioneering years of British aviation only a handful of years after the dawn of aviation itself.

The Pemberton-Billing Sojourn

It was in Southampton in October 1913 that Noel Pemberton-Billing, an eccentric inventor, property developer, motorist, yachtsman and aviation pioneer, set up a factory in co-operation with Hubert Scott-Paine, a motor-boat enthusiast, in a disused coal yard on the Woolston shore of the River Itchen to produce marine aircraft, with a ready-made 'runway' on the doorstep.

The imaginative and distinctive sobriquet 'Supermarine' was registered as the Company's telegraphic address. The opposite of submarine, it resulted from Pemberton-Billing's declared intention 'to build boats that fly rather than aeroplanes that float' – what today would be called a 'mission statement' – and they were to be known as 'Supermarines'. Although Supermarine was taken over by Vickers in 1928, the company retained this distinctive title throughout its life and continued to operate substantially autonomously in its own distinctive fashion until its ultimate demise in 1963.

The first machine was designated P.B.1 and was shown at the Olympia Aero Show in March 1914 – although it was never to fly – and the company was formally incorporated as Pemberton-Billing Limited on 17 June 1914. Shortly before the start of the First World War later that year, an order was received from the German Navy for two of its P.B.7s, a flying boat which could shed its wings when on water and proceed as an ordinary motor-boat, but this was cancelled with the outbreak of hostilities. Pemberton-Billing also obtained orders from the Admiralty for building aircraft designed by other firms. His own P.B.9 was called The Seven Day Bus because it was assembled in that number of days, but no orders were forthcoming. Other Pemberton-Billing designs included the P.B.23/25 for the Royal Naval Air Service and the ungainly P.B.29E, a quadruplane specially designed for attacking invading German Zeppelin airships.

When the British Government effectively took over the company for wartime purposes, Pemberton-Billing disagreed with the procurement policy of the Air Department for the Admiralty. In March 1916 he decided to enter Parliament in an attempt to change it, relinquishing his interest in the venture that he had founded after only two-and-a-half years at its head. The direction of the company was then taken over by his founding partner, Hubert Scott-Paine, who, because of Pemberton-Billing's mercurial character, had in reality been the driving force thus far. Then becoming known as The Supermarine Aviation Works Limited, it continued under Government control throughout the war and notably produced the first British flying-boat fighter, the biplane Baby.

The original Pemberton-Billing Works at Woolston in 1913 with Harry Foot, head carpenter and joiner, in the centre. An article in *The Southampton Times and Express* in November 1913 under the headline *Flying Factory at Itchen Ferry* read: 'Workers are engaged on a stretch of river frontage between Floating Bridge Hard and the old Ferry Yard (on the Woolston shore of the River Itchen near Southampton), preparing premises for the construction of Supermarine; there is already on the site one large shed once used as a coal wharf which has been converted into an engine building. A second shed 200 feet by 60 feet is now being constructed. Cottages in Elm Road, facing the site, are to be altered into offices, the river frontage up to the Floating Bridge Company's premises has been secured for the building of 'Water Planes'. Mr Pemberton-Billing, who boasted he would be given a flying certificate after twelve hours flying, actually gained it after three hours (at Brooklands). He is the proprietor of the venture, which is expected to be working by Christmas'.

The Genius of Reginald Mitchell

This was the situation when 22-year old Reginald Joseph Mitchell joined Supermarine in 1917 from his native Stoke-on-Trent, where he had served a five-year apprenticeship with Kerr Stuart, the well-known local firm of locomotive engineers – a classical engineering training at that time. During the next twenty years before his untimely death from cancer in June 1937 when only 42, he inspired a lineage of twenty-four different sea- and land-based commercial and military flying boats, together with a series of seaplane racers which triumphantly won World Air Speed Records and the prestigious Schneider Trophy outright for Britain in 1931. In turn, this led directly to his nation-saving Spitfire – widely-regarded as the world's most successful aircraft programme ever. Finally, he had also designed a heavy bomber, the emerging prototypes of which were unfortunately destroyed by enemy action soon after the outbreak of the Second World War.

Initially appointed as personal assistant to Scott-Paine, a period as assistant to the Works Manager followed before Reginald Mitchell succeeded Mr F.J. Hargreaves as Chief Designer in 1919 at the age of only 24. The Supermarine factory at that time consisted of a large hangar where the aircraft were built, with smaller buildings on either side for boat-building and offices, the design team comprising six draughtsmen and a secretary.

Back under its own control after the war, after converting some of the surplus Admiralty Air Department (A.D.) flying boats, which it had built during the war, into 'Channels' for commercial use, Supermarine began, at the end of 1920, to build civilian flying boats once more. Scott-Paine also became greatly attracted to competing for the internationally-prestigious Schneider Trophy, involving teams from the USA, Italy, France and Great Britain.

This award had originally been presented in 1913 by Jacques Schneider, the wealthy son of a French armaments manufacturer, who saw great potential for the seaplane in using the vast water-covered areas of the earth's surface as cheap airports. Presented to the nation demonstrating the fastest seaplane over a measured course, it was keenly contested in spectacular annual, and later biennial, events, the winning country having to stage the next race and the one ultimately achieving three successive victories being able to retain the Trophy.

The French had won the first event in 1913, with a British Sopwith seaplane winning the second contest shortly before the outbreak of war the following year. Discontinued during the war, the contest re-emerged in 1919, by which time Reginald Mitchell had become well-established at Supermarine and become universally and affectionately known as 'RJ'. With insufficient time to build a wholly-new machine, he converted the Supermarine Baby commercial flying boat into the Sea Lion – so named because it was powered by a 450 hp Napier Lion engine derived from motor-racing – as the company's first entrant. Flown off Bournemouth, the race turned out to be a fiasco. The Sea Lion suffered hull damage and, as no other competitor satisfactorily completed the course, the race was declared null and void.

In 1920, and also now promoted to Chief Engineer, Mitchell turned his attention to the British Government's specification for a new amphibian, with his Napier Lion-engined entry winning an £8,000 second prize. This was his first success with an aircraft for which he had been primarily responsible. Producing an improved version in 1921, which was first named Seal and later, Seagull, this type was built in quantity for the Royal Air Force which had been formed three years earlier, and the Royal Australian Air Force. It continued in service until the outbreak of the Second World War.

The 1920 and 1921 Schneider Trophy contests were held in Venice, with no British entries,

The Supermarine Works at Woolston in 1919 with the Pemberton-Billing yacht basin (left), the flying-boat works (right) and an A.D. (Admiralty Air Department) flying-boat ready for launching.

and both were won by Italy. Meanwhile, Scott-Paine began to consider a Supermarine entry for the 1922 event to be held at Naples, realising that the Italians now needed only one more win to claim the Trophy outright. There being no British Government support in prospect, the Sea Lion II was prepared in secret. Largely through the skill of Supermarine's Guernsey-born test pilot, Henri Biard, the Italian Macchi was narrowly beaten for the Trophy to be brought triumphantly back to Britain – a most commendable achievement for such a small company competing with what was essentially a standard commercial flying boat.

Scott-Paine left Supermarine in 1923 to develop high-speed motor-boats and Squadron Commander James Bird, who had joined the Company in 1919, took over. A new board of directors was appointed and Mitchell was given control of virtually all company work. His next design was the six-passenger Sea Eagle commercial biplane amphibian which was the first Supermarine aircraft to use RT (radio telecommunications) with the ground.

When the Supermarine Sea Lion III was roundly beaten in the 1923 Schneider Trophy contest off Cowes, Isle of Wight, by three specially-designed Curtiss seaplanes sponsored by the American Navy, Mitchell quickly realised that this marked the end of racing flying boats. It therefore raised the need for something really special if Britain was to have any chance of recapturing the Trophy.

This exceptional challenge marked a double milestone in his professional career. On the one hand, it led him to conceive a completely new racing seaplane series, the influence of which on British aviation and successive work at Supermarine in particular was to be profound. On the other, it also resulted in him signing an agreement with Supermarine to employ him as Chief Engineer and Designer for ten years and for him to be offered a technical directorship in 1927. The agreement also included provisions whereby he would continue to serve whatever new company resulted if Supermarine were to be wound up voluntarily for the purpose of reconstruction or amalgamation. So it was that Mitchell continued in this key position when Vickers took over Supermarine in November 1928 – a takeover thought to be devised mainly to secure his now exceptional abilities.

As well as considering the next Schneider Trophy entrant, Mitchell was bringing forward several other new commercial and military flying boat designs – notably the development of the Sea Lion into the Scarab, capable of carrying a 1,000 lb load, and twelve of which were sold to Spain for use in its war against Morocco. The Swan commercial amphibian of 1924 also incorporated an ingenious mechanism for retracting the undercarriage, activated by an air-driven propeller.

Winning the Schneider Trophy for Britain.

Whereas Mitchell had established a reputation for sound design with the Sea Lion amphibian lineage from 1922 and with the Southampton military flying boat of 1925 – one of the most successful aircraft in its class and in its time ever to be operated by the Royal Air Force – it was his famous 'S' (for Schneider) series of seaplane racers, conceived in Supermarine's determined battle to win the Schneider Trophy outright, which captured the imagination of the aviation world. Showing his now characteristic ingenuity and foresight at their

An early Supermarine Company emblem.

10

brilliant best, these sleek and very fast monoplane twin-float racing aircraft progressively incorporated such significant technical innovations as stressed-skin construction, tubular rods as control runs and wing trailing-edge flaps.

After the initial wooden-construction, Napier Lion-engined, S.4, which suffered aileron flutter in the 1925 contest held at Baltimore in the USA, but which won a World Speed Record of 226.75 mph over Southampton water, came the metal-construction S.5 which won the 1927 contest in Venice, and the S.6 which won at Calshot in 1929. However it was his ultimate Rolls-Royce powered S.6B which achieved the requisite third successive victory in 1931, again at Calshot, to enable the Trophy to be won outright for Britain – thanks also to the RAF High Speed Flight Team and to Lady Houston, the noted aviation philanthropist, who generously donated £100,000 in the absence of British Government support. The S.6B also went on to raise the World Air Speed Record to an incredible 407.02 mph, a speed that was not to be overtaken by fighter aircraft for another twenty years.

This triumphant conclusion to Supermarine's twelve-year saga to win the coveted Trophy continues to be celebrated as one of the greatest truimphs of British aeronautical history. It also enabled Mitchell to engage his ideas and talents in other more commercial directions for Supermarine.

While the Scapa replaced the Southampton, Nanok and Seamew commercial flying boat family, there was also the private venture Walrus single-engined biplane amphibian, first flown in 1934. This was to prove to be immensely valuable during the Second World War in the role of search and rescue of Allied aircrews ditched at sea.

A majestic trio of Scapas (originally designed as the Southampton IV) of Royal Air Force No. 202 (General Reconnaissance) Squadron over Alexandria Harbour, Egypt, flying from their base in Malta in 1935 and symbolising the impressive lineage of Supermarine military and commercial flying boats of the 1920s and early 1930s.

The Nation-Saving Spitfire

The last of Mitchell's beloved flying boats was the Stranraer, also in 1934, which left him free to begin his greatest work – the Spitfire.

Presciently realising the national significance of the threat of renewed confrontation in Europe, he focused his attention on the Air Ministry specification F.7/30 for a single-seat, single-engined, monoplane fighter (his first design in this category). However, he was convinced that his resulting Type 224 was but a stepping stone to something substantially better and considerably more potent.

Against strong opposition from almost every quarter of officialdom, Mitchell was staunchly supported by Sir Robert Maclean, the forceful Chairman of Vickers (Aviation) Ltd. As Sir Robert said in an article in the *Sunday Times* in 1957: 'I felt that (Mitchell's) design team would do much better by devoting their qualities not to the official experimental fighter (F.7/30) but to a real killer fighter. After unfruitful discussions with the Air Ministry, my opposite number in Rolls-Royce, the late A.F. Sidgreaves and I, decided that the two companies should themselves finance the building of such an aircraft. The Air Ministry was informed of the decision and were told that in no circumstances would any technical member of the Air Ministry be consulted or allowed to interfere with the designer.' Consequently, with the wealth of aerodynamic experience gained through the Schneider Trophy racers, Mitchell set about the conception of a superior eight-gun fighter, a monoplane with retracting undercarriage and powered by the Rolls-Royce PV12 engine, later to become the famous Merlin, and around which the Air Ministry specification F.37/34 was especially written.

The full and extraordinary success story of the Spitfire has been well and widely chronicled and is clear testimony not only to the genius of Mitchell but also to the diligence of Joe Smith, his indefatigable successor as Chief Designer, and the entire Supermarine team when faced with the most formidable wartime exigencies. Their spirit and ingenuity in overcoming horrendous enemy action in September 1940, and instituting urgent large-scale production dispersal and continuous development, was exemplary. Together with the equally-determined efforts of Rolls-Royce, they enabled the Spitfire to be maintained at the forefront of allied aerial supremacy, over land and at sea, throughout the Second World War, wherever the need was greatest.

The nation-saving role of the Vickers-Supermarine Spitfire (together with Sydney Camm's Hawker Hurricane) in the greatest-ever air battle, The Battle of Britain, is a perennial highlight of military aviation history.

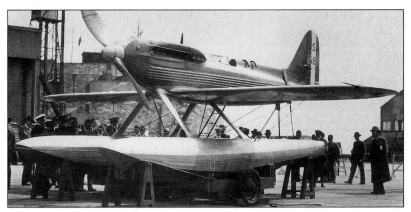

The admiration of excellence – the Supermarine S6B S1595 racing seaplane – ultimate winner of the Schneider Trophy outright for Britain in 1931. This famous aircraft and Trophy are today proudly displayed together at the Science Museum in South Kensington, London.

War and Pieces

When the prototype Spitfire K5054 was being assembled in a restricted area in one of the erecting shops at Woolston in 1936, Supermarine's production products were the Walrus and the Stranraer, with a staff of about 500 people.

The Spitfire was Supermarine's first major landplane programme, hence the need for a suitable airfield. Eastleigh Airport was a natural choice and the first flight was made there by 'Mutt' Summers, Vickers' Chief Test Pilot, on Thursday 5 March 1936, sixty years ago this year (1996). When the initial order for 310 production Spitfires came only two months later, it was clear that a whole new production concept would be needed.

In 1939, when the outbreak of war was imminent, subcontractors for major airframe components were engaged throughout the country and a dispersal scheme devised in the Southampton area by the requisitioning of a bus station and three sizeable garages to support the two main Spitfire production centres, Woolston and Itchen, with the final assembly and flight testing at Eastleigh. Unfortunately, the strategic importance of Southampton, together with its well-known location and close proximity to enemy air bases after the fall of France, meant that it was particularly vulnerable to air attack.

While Churchill's brave young 'Few' were so courageously defending the English skies with their Spitfires and Hurricanes in September 1940, concentrated German bombing raids badly damaged the Itchen works and the Woolston works and offices – on 24 and 26 September 1940 respectively – with more than one hundred people losing their lives. A devastating blitz of the town of Southampton followed shortly afterwards. Lord Beaverbrook, the ebullient Minister of Aircraft Production (MAP), immediately ordered a complete dispersal of the entire Supermarine works and the Spitfire production programme in the Southampton area and across the South of England. The fourth floor of the Polygon Hotel, near the Southampton Civic Centre, was requisitioned by the MAP, and the Supermarine management team immediately began planning this most complex operation.

The much-modernised Supermarine factory c. 1937-40 at the time of the early build-up of Spitfire production and before the disastrous bombing in September 1940.

Meanwhile, the design office was moved to part of the University College of Southampton and the commercial office to a large private house, Deepdene, at Bitterne Park. With large-scale Ordnance Survey maps of Hampshire, Wiltshire and Berkshire, a master plan was drawn up centred on five towns with adjacent aerodromes: the Southampton area using Eastleigh, Salisbury using High Post (and later also Chattis Hill racing gallops), Trowbridge using Keevil, with Newbury and Reading initially using Henley and later, Aldermaston.

Wing and fuselage assembly jigs were installed at each of the five centres for these major assemblies to be married together at the aerodromes, with five final assembly lines instead of the previous one. The piece-part and sub-assembly manufacturing stages were again sub-divided and transferred to a large number of requisitioned local premises – large motor garages, bus stations, laundries and large store premises. To operate this huge and widely dispersed organisation, Commander (later Sir) James Bird, the man who had sold Supermarine to Vickers in 1928, was made Supermarine's General Manager. Len Gooch, the architect of the whole plan, was made Works Manager, with five area managers and a total of 9,600 employees responsible to him.

In the six weeks after the bombing in 1940, 35 different units were being converted, 16 were working day- and night-shifts and the balance in the initial planning were ready for operation a short time afterwards. Eventually, the entire Spitfire production programme was spread over 65 different units, the total production floor area being increased from 230,400 sq ft prior to the bombing, to 1,385,000 sq ft when the dispersal was fully operational. Between them, the units built more than 8,500 aircraft. The Southampton dispersal complex was the largest of the five and comprised 28 locations employing around 3,000 people.

In December 1940, the Supermarine administration and technical design offices moved to a country mansion at Hursley Park, near Winchester, the home of Lady Cooper, where a new drawing office and an experimental shop were later erected in the grounds. Hursley Park became the control centre of the entire Spitfire and Seafire development programme for the duration of the war under the leadership of the redoubtable Joe Smith, who had succeeded Reginald Mitchell on his tragic and untimely death in 1937.

Meanwhile, Jeffrey Quill, who had taken over from 'Mutt' Summers soon after the maiden flight, led the Spitfire flight test team throughout the entire decade-long development programme, including active service in the Battle of Britain and the Fleet Air Arm to obtain first-hand appreciation of operational requirements and problems.

The largest Spitfire production unit, responsible for more than half the total output of 22,749 aircraft, was the

Of the countless thousands of photographs of the immortal Vickers-Supermarine Spitfire, this is probably the most evocative action shot ever. It shows Spitfire F.MkXIV RB140 being flown by Supermarine's renowned Chief Test Pilot, Jeffrey Quill, and was taken through the side-door of an Airspeed Oxford by Supermarine photographer Frank Burr. The Oxford was being flown by Supermarine Test Pilot, Frank Furlong, a former steeplechase jockey who had won the 1935 Grand National.

14

Government-owned Shadow factory at Castle Bromwich, near Birmingham. Directly under the control of Supermarine's parent company, Vickers-Armstrongs Ltd., it reached a peak of 320 aircraft a week in June 1944 under the leadership of Bonner 'Dick' Dickson, with Alex Henshaw leading the correspondingly-large flight-testing programme. Large batches of Seafires were also made by Westland at Yeovil and by Cunliffe-Owen, adjacent to Supermarine, at Eastleigh. This huge unit also had its own satellites, one of which was at South Marston, near Swindon, Wiltshire, from where some of the last Mks Spitfire and Seafire issued.

Into the Jet Age and the Final Years

Hursley Park continued as the headquarters of Supermarine in the post-war period when the Spitfire/Seafire piston-engined genus gave way to the jet age and was succeeded by three generations of Supermarine jet fighters – the Attacker, the Royal Navy's first jet aircraft; the Swift, the first British swept-wing aircraft for the Royal Air Force, which also won a World Air Speed Record in 1953, and ultimately the big carrier-borne Scimitar fighter, the Royal Navy's first swept-wing jet aircraft. Supermarine also engaged in pioneering work on Hovercraft and on 20 July 1962 the world's first commercial Hovercraft service was operated between Wallasey and Rhyl in North Wales, by the Vickers VA-3.

South Marston was subsequently acquired by Vickers to become the ultimate Supermarine headquarters and where the jet fighter final assembly was located with flight testing being carried out at Chilbolton in Hampshire.

Supermarine design in its own right finally came to an end in 1957 when the office at Hursley Park was closed and the bulk of the staff transferred either to South Marston for work on non-aviation projects or to the main Vickers-Armstrongs (Aircraft) design organisation at Weybridge in Surrey, where they continued to contribute to the design of the TSR2 supersonic bomber project, to which they had already made a primary input, also utilising their valuable experience in advanced military and naval fighter projects.

This outstanding little company had thus sustained its original dedication to marine aircraft as a central theme thoughout its entire fifty years of operation – from Pemberton-Billing's P.B.1 of 1913/1914 through to the completion of the last Scimitar at South Marston in 1963.

Supermarine's other notorious Second World War aircraft – the indefatigable Walrus air-sea rescue amphibian that was responsible for saving the lives of very many ditched Allied airmen.

Legacy and Epitaph

Now a third of a century on, since disappearing from the British aviation scene, in this the sixtieth anniversary year of the first flight of the world-renowned Spitfire, the distinctive name and the exceptional accomplishments of Supermarine and its legendary designer, Reginald Mitchell, are especially remembered and revered.

The Supermarine epoch spanned half a century of the highest aeronautical standard-setting and achievement, embracing critical and demanding times and two World Wars. From laying the foundations of global marine aviation, winning world acclaim in racing and record-breaking, providing a decisive instrument of national defence in the darkest hours of need, and through to the age of the jet engine, swept wings and the threshold of supersonic flight, the achievements of the Company constituted an extremely proud and honourable legacy and epitaph.

Today, this is most physically evident at the R.J. Mitchell Memorial Museum in the Southampton Hall of Aviation and several Supermarine aircraft types are also preserved around the country. The hard-won Schneider Trophy and the victorious S.6B are still proudly displayed at the Science Museum in London. More than 200 Spitfires are also preserved around the world, forty-six of them remaining airworthy, exactly half in the UK.

Good reason, therefore, why its modern-day successors – Vickers, British Aerospace and indeed the entire British aviation industry – should continue to be proud to count Supermarine among their illustrious founding predecessors. They owe it much for bequeathing them with such an exceptional and valuable heritage.

The last of the fifty-year lineage of Supermarines – the big Vickers-Supermarine twin-jet naval fighter, the Royal Navy's first swept-wing jet aircraft. Scimitars were flown from the Royal Navy aircraft carriers HMS *Ark Royal, Centaur, Eagle, Hermes* and *Victorious*. The last Scimitar left the South Marston factory in 1963 and marked the end of the illustrious fifty-year story of the Company while also maintaining its original and primary dedication to marine aircraft throughout that time.

One

The Pemberton-Billing Sojourn

Noel Pemberton-Billing, one of the earliest yet least remembered British aviation entrepreneurs, had the distinction not only of founding, in October 1913, what went on to become one of the world's most accomplished aircraft manufacturing companies, but also of giving his fledgling aviation business venture a clear and distinct objective – marine aircraft – and locating it in an ideal place in which his aspirations could best be realised.

In so doing, he can also be credited with inventing what was to become one of the most appropriate and enduring of all aeronautical company names – Supermarine. Several orders were secured and diverse and inventive designs quickly emerged to bear the P.B. prefix and become known as 'Supermarines'.

However, after only a two-and-a-half-year sojourn, his restless and mercurial character led to a disagreement with the Air Department over war work for the Admiralty and resulted in his abrupt departure into the political arena in March 1916. Leaving the Company in the capable hands of his founding partner, Hubert Scott-Paine, thereafter it sensibly reverted from Pemberton-Billing Limited to become famously known as The Supermarine Aviation Works Limited.

Noel Pemberton-Billing, founding father of Supermarine, with Robert Barnwell of the Vickers Flying School at Brooklands on 17 September 1913 when P-B bought a Farman and learned to fly in one day, before breakfast, to win a wager of £500 from Frederick Handley Page and be awarded Aviator's Certificate No. 632.

Pemberton-Billing in his Farman at Brooklands with the world's first flight booking office (centre); part of the world's first closed-circuit, banked motor-racing track (background); and the Flying School and the Blue Bird restaurant – which was owned and operated by Eardley Billing, P-B's brother (right).

Pemberton-Billing with his first aircraft, the Supermarine P.B.1 biplane flying boat, at its first public appearance at the Olympia Aero Show in March 1914.

The P.B.1 being man-handled prior to launching at Woolston on the River Itchen.

The P.B.1 being launched at Woolston after modification in 1914 to incorporate two wing-mounted, chain-driven, three-bladed, pusher propellers. The Company's telegraphic address on the factory shed is written 'Supermarin', without the final 'e', presumably because for that purpose it was limited to ten characters.

P-B taxying the modified P.B.1 on the River Itchen in May/June 1914. It failed to fly.

Final assembly of the P.B.9 Seven Day Bus – so called because it was built in that many days – before its first test flight on 12 August 1914. Powered by a 50 hp gnome engine, it reached a top speed of 78 mph and a rate of climb of 500 ft/min.

PEMBERTON-BILLING

FLYING.

ILLUSTRATIONS DEMONSTRATING THE LATEST TYPE OF

"SUPERMARINE"
(FLYING LIFEBOAT)

BUILT UNDER PEMBERTON-BILLING PATENTS AT HIS
SOUTHAMPTON WORKS.

ON THE WATER AND WINGS DETACHED.

SOUTHAMPTON—ENGLAND.

Pemberton-Billing/Supermarine advertisement in *Flight* magazine of 29 May 1914 showing an impression of P-B's patented P.B.7 slip-wing flying boat (incorporating nose-mounted gun) and designed to proceed as a motor-boat with underwater propeller in case of emergency.

The remarkable little 20 ft span P.B.9 Seven Day Bus with (left to right): Hubert Scott-Paine, Pemberton-Billing's founding partner, Victor Mahl, the pilot, and C. Vasilesco, design draughtsman.

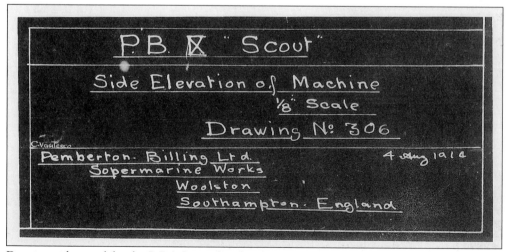

Drawing title panel for the P.B.9 Scout dated 4 August 1914 with the draughtsman's name, C. Vasilesco, half way up the left-hand side.

Although the P.B.9 did not enter production, it served as a trainer with the Royal Naval Air Service (RNAS) at Hendon and is reputed still to have been in service in 1918.

The P.B.9 flying over the Bleriot Works at Addlestone in Surrey.

Noel Pemberton-Billing campaigning from his P.B.9 Seven Day Bus aircraft in London's Mile End parliamentary elections in January 1916.

A Pusher Type Fighting Scout designed & built for A.D. Admiralty early in 1915.

Advertising material in 1915 for the straight-winged P.B.23E Push-Proj and eleven-degree sweepback P.B.25 Fighting Scouts – the suffix 'E' standing for Experimental as in the Government-designed B.E., R.E. and S.E. series of military aircraft and other contemporary designs.

The P.B.23E Push-Proj with modified fins of the type later fitted to the P.B.25.

The first production P.B.25 (9001) with a 110 hp Clerget engine.

P.B.25 9002 powered by a 100 hp Gnome Monosoupape engine showing the 11-degree sweepback of the wings to adjust the centre of gravity.

Another view of P.B.25 9002, the second of twenty such aircraft produced. None were used operationally, although the type was flown at Eastchurch, the Isle of Grain and Killingholme.

P.B.25 9004 at Guston Road Royal Naval Air Station (RNAS) Dover in 1916 'on test for defence'.

Seven production P.B.25 fuselages at various stages of completion, the first two with the wooden monocoque construction uncovered.

The P.B. 29E Zeppelin Destroyer quadruplane powered by two tractor Austro-Daimler engines shortly before it crashed on its first flight. The large wing area and high aspect-ratio were to promote the slow and high flying necessary to combat the German airship menace.

The P.B.31E Nighthawk improved version of the P.B.29E showing the star-shaped louvres in the nose which admitted cooling air to the auxiliary power unit for a searchlight also located in this position. The armament consisted of large Davis guns in the nose, beam and 'fighting-top' positions.

Two
The Genius of
Reginald Mitchell

Reginald Joseph ('RJ') Mitchell played a decisive role in the conception of twenty-four different Supermarine aircraft types in just twenty years before his premature death at 42, thus qualifying him to be rated as the most versatile of all British aircraft designers and a true genius. Working in a period of enormous technical change and during both adventurous and critical times, he proved to be the right man for both.

Joining the fledgling Supermarine at Southampton in 1917 at the age of 22 and becoming Chief Designer two years later, his next twelve years were dominated by Supermarine's determined aspiration to win the internationally-prestigious Schneider Trophy for Britain. This it did in spectacular style with his brilliant seaplane racers between 1925 and 1931, while simultaneously realising his impressive range of commercial and military seaplanes.

The acquisition of Supermarine by Vickers in November 1928 was largely to acquire Mitchell's outstanding abilities and was amply vindicated. His most enduring monument, the Spitfire, resulted from a unique combination of flair and courage when facing terminal illness. Although he only saw the prototype, first airborne on 5 March 1936, when he died fifteen months later, he knew that it was already an assured success.

Reginald Joseph ('RJ') Mitchell, CBE, FRAeS, AMICE, 1895–1937: Britain's most versatile aircraft designer and one of the great British heroes of engineering and of the twentieth century.

Hubert Scott-Paine (right) and an Admiralty overseer with the Supermarine AD Navyplane
built for the Admiralty Air Department during the First World War.

The Supermarine N.1B Baby single-seat flying-boat fighter designed by F.J. Hargreaves and
assisted by Reginald Mitchell. This single-bay biplane had a Linton-Hope type hull, folding
wings for shipboard stowage, and a pusher propeller driven by a geared 200 hp Hispano engine.
The single example N59 achieved 117 mph at sea level and in August 1918, with a Sunbeam
Arab engine, reached 111.5 mph at 10,000 ft. This was the first Supermarine aircaft type with
which Mitchell was identified.

Reginald Mitchell with contemporaries of the Supermarine Works team when he joined the Company at the age of 22 in 1917, initially as personal assistant to Hubert Scott-Paine, who had by then taken over the ownership of the Company from its founder, Noel Pemberton-Billing. Scott-Paine is fifth from left in the back row (wearing hat) and Mitchell is third from the right. On his right is Miss Lyall, Head of the Dope Shop, and next to her is Mr F.J. Hargreaves, Chief of the Design Department, whom Mitchell succeeded in 1919. Second from left is Sqn. Ldr. Basil Hobbs, who piloted the Supermarine Sea Lion in the 1919 Schneider Trophy race; on his left is Mr Leach, Works Superintendent, to whom Mitchell was assistant for a short period before becoming Chief Designer. In the front row (left to right) are Arthur Nelson, Head Rigger, who managed the Southampton dispersal complex after the bombing of the Supermarine factories at Woolston and Itchen in 1940, Mr Boyce, Woodmill, Mr V. Dartnell, Engine Department, and Mr W.T. Elliott, Works Manager, who became Works Superintendent of the whole of the Supermarine dispersal programme in the South of England during the Second World War.

Supermarine Channel I mail- and passenger-carrying flying-boat (ex G-EAEH and N1716) sold as N9 to the Royal Norwegian Navy in May 1920. A postal service between Christiania and Christiansand was also opened with four of these machines on 12 July 1920. The Channels were surplus wartime A.D. Boats repurchased by Supermarine in 1919, initially for the conversion of ten of them for flying trips from Southampton to seaside resorts in the Isle of Wight. A shortage of pilots led to the recruitment from the former Royal Naval Air Service, notably including James Bird, who later became General Manager of the Company, and Guernsey-born Henri Biard, who became Supermarine's first Chief Test Pilot.

Supermarine Channel for a Venezuelan expedition on the Woolston slipway after passing trials. Other Channels were sold to Bermuda, the Imperial Japanese Navy, the Royal Swedish Navy, British Guiana and Chile – an impressive early export achievement.

The Supermarine Commercial Amphibian G-EAVE entry for the Air Ministry amphibian competition at Martlesham Heath, Suffolk, in 1920. Powered by a 350 hp Rolls-Royce Eagle VIII engine, it won second prize of £8,000. This was Mitchell's first success with an aircraft for which he had been primarily responsible.

G-EAVE nearing completion with Harry Foot, Supermarine's head carpenter and joiner, by the nose with five two-gallon petrol cans at the ready.

Supermarine Sea Eagle six-passenger, enclosed cabin amphibian powered by a 360 hp Rolls-Royce Eagle IX pusher engine. G-EBGS, the third of three built for the British Marine Air Navigation Company to operate between Southampton, Cherbourg, Le Havre and the Channel Islands, at the Woolston terminal in Imperial Airways livery as the eventual operator in 1924.

The christening of the Sea Eagle G-EBGS Sarnia at St Peter Port harbour, Guernsey, by Miss Edith Carey and Mrs Watkin, wife of the Senior Constable of St Peter Port, in 1923.

The Supermarine Sea King II G-EBAH single-seat military amphibian fighter of 1921 powered by a 300 hp Hispano-Suiza pusher engine and developed from the N.1B Baby via the Sea King I high-speed flying-boat that was powered by a 160 hp Beardmore engine. This was the first complete Supermarine aircraft design over which Reginald Mitchell had full authority as Chief Designer, and this extended to the modifications necessary when the type was considered as an entry for the 1922 Schneider Trophy contest at Naples, for which it was renamed Sea Lion II.

The Supermarine Seal Mk.II (the short-lived Commercial Amphibian was regarded as the Seal Mk.I) at Woolston in 1921. Designed by Mitchell as a three-seat, deck-landing amphibian, N146 incorporated a modified balanced rudder after directional control difficulties. The final rudder outline survived into later versions of the Seagull – as the Seal was renamed on 4 July 1922.

The first of six Napier Lion-engined Supermarine Seagull amphibians for survey work in Australia being made ready at Southampton for the official launch by Lady Cook, wife of Sir Joseph Cook, the Australian High Commissioner in London in February 1926.

M-NSAA, the first of twelve Supermarine Scarab amphibian flying boats – the military version of the Sea Eagle – built during 1924 for the Spanish Navy in its war against Morocco. Based on the Sea Eagle, it was fitted with a 360 hp Rolls-Royce Eagle IX engine and carried a maximum bomb load of 1,000 lb.

A diversion from Mitchell's basic flying-boat lineage, the Supermarine Sparrow I light sesquiplane, with a 35hp Blackburn Thrush engine, designed to compete in the Two-Seater Light Aeroplane Competition held at Lympne, Kent, in September/October 1924 with an Air Ministry prize of £2,000 for 'the best lightplane designed and built in Great Britain'. Plagued by engine failures, it was not successful. The competition was won by the Hawker Cygnet. The Sparrow also competed for the Steward's Prize, which was for the eliminated aircraft, and in the Grosvenor Cup Race, but was unplaced in both.

In 1927, under an Air Ministry contract, the Sparrow II braced parasol monoplane version, powered by a Bristol Cherub, was used to investigate full-scale the merits of four different contemporary aerofoil sections.

The little-known Supermarine Sheldrake N-180 of 1927 was apparently an experimental development of the Seagull and Scarab, with revised hull lines and powered by a 450 hp Napier Lion V engine.

Supermarine's first twin-engined flying-boat built to the world's first twin-engined amphibian requirement 21/22, the Supermarine Swan, was the result of the second of two separate contracts. The first, placed in 1921, was for a five-seat military flying-boat and named Scylla but the fate of which is unknown. That for the Swan, and placed in 1922, was for a commercial amphibian. N-175 (later registered G-EBJY) carried ten passengers, with baggage, for 300 miles at a cruising speed of 92 mph and was operated for a time on the Channel Islands service as a back-up for the Sea Eagle.

HRH Edward Prince of Wales (centre in uniform) in front of the Supermarine Swan amphibian at the time of his visit to the Supermarine Works in 1924. Third from right is Reginald Mitchell, fourth is Henri Biard, Supermarine's Chief Test Pilot, and fifth is Sqn. Cdr. James Bird, General Manager.

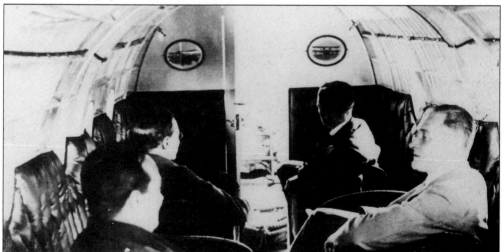

Reginald Mitchell (right) seated in the commonly-used wicker-type chairs in the cabin of the Supermarine Swan amphibian. The real significance of the Swan experimental design was that it became the precursor of one of most successful of all of Mitchell's diverse marine aircraft lineage, the Supermarine Southampton military flying-boat, of which a total of eighty-three were ultimately built (seventy-nine plus four prototypes).

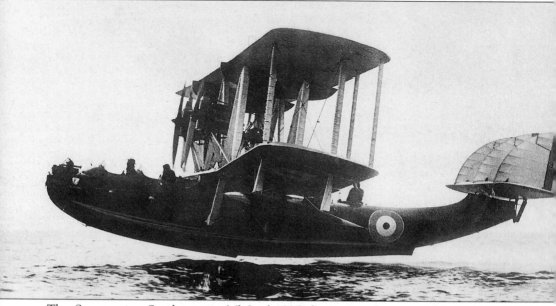

The Supermarine Southampton Mk.I of 1925, beginning the series that was to set new standards in marine aircraft, at the point of touchdown on the Solent water. The wooden-hulled Mk.I proved itself in 1926 by making cruises in formation. This notably included a twenty-day cruise by four aircraft of 10,000 miles around the British Isles together with exercises with the Royal Navy in the Irish Sea. There was also one cruise of nearly 7,000 miles by two aircraft in the Mediterranean from Plymouth and back. A new feature of this long-distance flight was that the aircraft were in constant touch with land bases by W/T (wireless telegraphy).

The wooden-hulled Southampton Mk.I during construction with two 450 hp Napier Lion engines mounted on pylons, independent of the Warren-type centre section, thus enabling maintenance or engine change without disturbance to the main wing structure.

One of eight Southampton Mk.Is delivered during 1927 to the Argentine Naval Air Force. Powered by two 450 hp Lorraine 12E engines, five of them were wooden-hulled (of which this is one) and three were metal-hulled. The wooden and metal hulls were identical dimensionally.

Supermarine Southampton N218, the experimental version built to Air Ministry Specification R.18/24 with a metal hull as the prototype Mk.II. The Duralumin hull was anodically-treated against corrosion and the basic structure was 540 lb lighter than that of the Mk.I. Elimination of water seepage permitted a further 400 lb of fuel to be carried and the range to be increased from 600 miles to nearly 900 miles.

Southampton Mk.II S1232, one of a batch of nine aircraft ordered in December 1926 and delivered to the Royal Air Force in 1927. Of these, S1235 was used temporarily by Imperial Airways as G-AASH.

A formation of Supermarine Southamptons at the Royal Air Force display at Hendon in 1930. The first three aircraft are Mk.Is built in 1926 and the fourth aircraft is a Mk.II, built in 1927.

One of the four Supermarine Southampton Mk.IIs of the Far East Flight of the Royal Air Force overland between Akyab and Rangoon, Burma, during a pioneering expedition in 1927-1928 to open up routes to the Far East and Australia and to gather information on potential seaplane bases, harbours and local conditions affecting maritime aircraft operation.

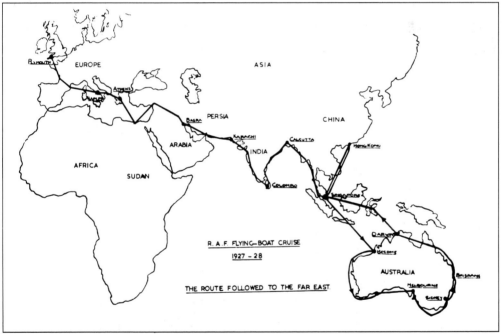

The route followed to the Far East by four Royal Air Force Southampton Mk.II flying-boats in 1927-1928. These aircraft flew a total of 23,000 miles in formation by way of Syria to Basra, down the Persian Gulf to Karachi, on to Calcutta, and through the East Indies to Australia. They then circled the entire continent of Australia, returning to Singapore, followed by a trip to Hong Kong, and finally took up station at Singapore. This outstandingly-successful mission was commanded by Group Captain Cave-Brown-Cave (who later became Professor of Engineering at University College, Southampton, and the founding President of the Southampton Branch of the Royal Aeronautical Society). It aroused world interest, adding greatly to the prestige of the British aircraft industry and to the already highly-regarded reputation of Supermarine and Reginald Mitchell.

Royal Air Force Southampton Mk.IIs S1233 and S1234 in formation.

Supermarine Southampton N252, the prototype Southampton X three-engined sesquiplane with a wider-span upper wing, being launched on the Woolston slipway, was one of three experimental aircraft ordered in June 1928 and built as Southampton Mk.Xs fitted with three 570 hp Bristol Jupiter XFBM engines.

Supermarine Southampton Mk.X N252 moored at anchor on the Solent. While the hull of this aircraft was the responsiblity of Supermarine itself, the wing superstructure, including the engine mountings, was entrusted to Vickers at Weybridge, which had recently become associated with Woolston in the Vickers (Aviation) merger of the two companies in 1928.

The Southampton Mk.II ordered for the Japanese Navy and delivered during 1928. It was subsequently converted to an eighteen-seat airliner, registered J-BAID and operated by Japan Air Transport on the Osaka-Beppu route in the 1930s. The commercial side of the purchase was handled by Mitsubishi.

The Vickers-Supermarine Southampton Mk.X of 1930, the ultimate development of this highly-successful military flying-boat family and powered by three Armstrong Siddeley Panther engines. The hull was flat-sided to facilitate production and its under-water portion was plated with stainless steel.

N212, the first of two Vickers-Supermarine Seamew military biplane three-seat reconnaissance amphibians. Powered by two Armstrong Siddeley Jaguars and tested at Felixstowe, with a span of 37 ft its appearance was akin to a half-scale Southampton. The Seamew was Mitchell's first attempt in metal construction to any extent.

Reginald Mitchell and Henri Biard, Supermarine's Chief Test Pilot, approaching the Seamew N212 on the Woolston factory slipway apron.

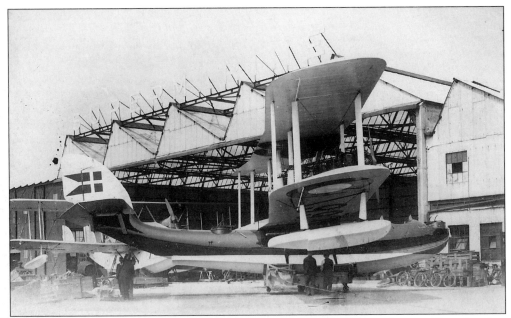

The Vickers-Supermarine Nanok development of the Southampton and originally ordered in 1928 by the Danish Navy as a torpedo carrier, hence its unusual name and the tail flash. Not delivered, it was later renamed Solent, after conversion to a private yacht for the Hon. A.E. Guinness and registered G-AAAB, in which form it gave many years of excellent service.

The Nanok on its launching trolley at Woolston and still in Danish navy guise with torpedo mounted.

After flying the Solent (nee Nanok), The Hon. A.E. Guinness placed an order for a further air yacht to his own specification, which was designed by Mitchell and built at Hythe in 1929. Registered G-AASE, this aircraft was a departure from Mitchell's previous flying-boats, being a three-engined parasol monoplane in which sponsons were used instead of wing-tip floats.

Mitchell's first multi-engined monoplane, the Vickers-Supermarine Air Yacht was powered by three Armstrong Siddeley geared Jaguar, and later Panther, engines mounted in the leading edge of the wing. The hull was luxuriously appointed for cruising with sleeping accommodation.

49

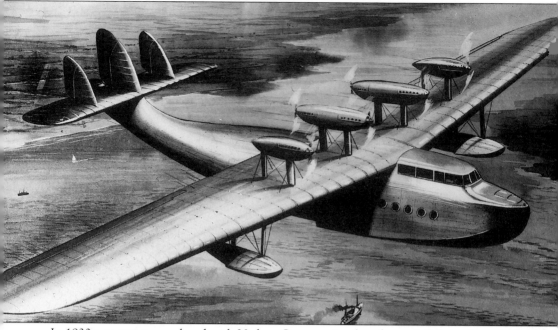

In 1930 a contract was placed with Vickers-Supermarine for a large civil flying-boat similar in size to the German Dornier Do X. Much of the design and construction work was completed when the Government cancelled it, at the end of 1931, on the grounds of economy. This ambitious design was to have been a six-engined flying-boat weighing 75,000 lb, powered by Rolls-Royce H (later the 1,030 hp Buzzard) engines, capable of carrying forty passengers with sleeping accommodation for twenty.

The hull of the Vickers-Supermarine Type 179 under construction. Registered G-ABLE on 7 April 1931, the keel was laid shortly afterwards and the aircraft was appropriately called Giant.

Designed by Mitchell in 1932 as a replacement for the Southampton, under construction and initially known as the Southampton Mk.IV, the Type 221 was later named Scapa. Powered by two under-wing mounted 525 hp Rolls-Royce Kestrel engines, the 75 ft span biplane amphibian had a hull larger than that of the Southampton; fifteen were built for the Royal Air Force.

The Vickers-Supermarine Scapa flying over Netley, near Southampton.

Originally known as the Seagull Mk.V, the renowned Vickers-Supermarine Walrus single 625 hp Bristol Pegasus IIM2 pusher engine amphibian which began life in 1933 as a private venture design for use on capital ships, and was accordingly fitted with catapult gear.

The prototype Vickers-Supermarine Type 223 Seagull Mk.V N-2 at the Marine Aircraft Experimental Establishment (MAEE) at Felixstowe, Suffolk, at the end of July 1933 for Air Ministry trials. Previously labelled N-1, Vickers Chief Test Pilot, 'Mutt' Summers, had perfomed aerobatics with this aircraft at the Society of British Aircraft Constructors (SBAC) Show at Hendon earlier that year.

The Seagull Mk.V prototype with wings folded for shipboard stowage.

The prototype Seagull Mk.V N-2 undergoing catapult trials at the Royal Aircraft Establishment (RAE), Farnborough, Hampshire, in February 1934.

The Seagull Mk.V on the catapult of HMAS *Sydney* of the Royal Australian Navy.

A2-1, the first of twenty-four Vickers-Supermarine Seagull Mk.V for the Royal Australian Air Force. This aircraft was also used in 1935 for trials with Bristol Pegasus IIM2 engines and Handley Page-type auto-slots on the upper wings.

The first production Vickers-Supermarine Type 236 Walrus K5772 which was first flown by George Pickering, the Company's well-known seaplane test pilot, on 18 March 1936.

K5772 at touchdown during trials in 1936. The signature in the bottom right corner is that of George Pickering.

The versatile Vickers-Supermarine Walrus, commonly-known in military service as the 'Shagbat', landing on board the aircraft carrier HMS *Sheffield*.

Of the several Walrus amphibians subsequently converted and used for civil purposes at home and abroad, PH-NAX was deployed by the Amsterdam Whaling Company. Another Walrus civil adaptation was that for United Whalers Ltd. of London. Walrus L2301, which was originally sold to Eire as N-18, saw service with the Irish airline Aer Lingus as EI-ACC before being rescued from scrap and renovated during the 1960s by the Royal Naval Air Station at Yeovilton, where it is now on display at the Fleet Air Arm Museum.

A Vickers-Supermarine Walrus being winched aboard HMS *Devonshire*. A total of 746 Walrus military general-purpose, reconnaissance, training and air-sea rescue amphibians were built between 1940 and 1944, in two basic versions, and supplied to the Royal Air Force, the Fleet Air Arm, the Royal New Zealand Air Force, the Royal Australian Navy and the Royal Canadian Navy.

The prototype Vickers-Supermarine Type 309 Sea Otter K8854 tractor development of the Walrus, first flown in September 1938, showing the initially-tried 'scissors' solution to the conflicting claims of propeller thrust and aircraft stowage height. Like the Walrus, the Sea Otter was quantity-produced under licence by Saunders-Roe (290 aircraft) for the Royal Air Force and the Fleet Air Arm, between 1943 and 1946.

A Royal Navy Sea Otter equipped with tail arrester hook and landing on a carrier deck.

The prototype Vickers-Supermarine Type 237 Stranraer K3973 multi-purpose military flying-boat, the last of Mitchell's large biplane flying-boats and originally called the Southampton MK.V. Developed from the Scapa, the Stranraer was powered by two Bristol Pegasus engines, had a larger hull and all-round improved performance. After trials, K3973 joined Royal Air Force No. 210 Squadron.

A trio of Royal Air Force Coastal Command Stranraer North Sea 'fleet watchdog' flying-boats setting out on patrol.

Of the fifty-eight Stranraers made, forty were licence-built by Canadian Vickers for the Royal Canadian Air Force for anti-submarine and convoy patrol, of which fourteen were given civil registrations. This one – CF-BXO *Alaska Queen* – served with Queen Charlotte Airlines (later Pacific Western Airlines) during the Second World War at Vancouver: it is now preserved at the Royal Air Force Museum at Hendon, North London.

A Royal Canadian Air Force Stranraer being launched at an Eastern Canadian port. When it came to deciding the shape of the fin and rudder for the Vickers B.9/32 Wellington prototype at Weybridge in 1936, 'Mutt' Summers, Vickers Chief Test Pilot, liked that of the Stranraer and so it was initially adopted in enlarged form for the bomber.

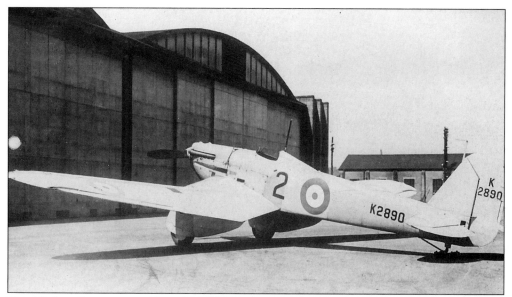

The Vickers-Supermarine Type 224 K2890 designed by Mitchell as his first foray into the fighter field, but to the mediocre Air Ministry F.7/30 specification, and first flown by 'Mutt' Summers, Vickers Chief Test Pilot, at Eastleigh on 19 February 1934. With its cranked gull wing and fixed trousered undercarriage, it was known as 'Spitfire' before that most famous of all aircraft names was officially adopted for the definitive and radically redesigned Type 300.

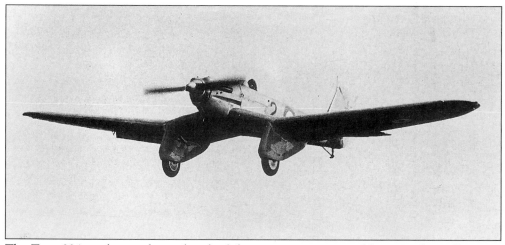

The Type 224 single-seat day and night fighter prototype, powered by a 600 hp Rolls-Royce Goshawk steam-cooled engine, as it appeared at the Royal Air Force display at Hendon in 1934.

The famous Vickers-Supermarine F.37/34 Type 300 prototype Spitfire K5054, shortly before its first flight by Captain Joseph 'Mutt' Summers, Vickers renowned Chief Test Pilot, at Eastleigh, on the morning of Thursday 5 March 1936, sixty years ago this year (1996) and a defining moment in British aviation. In the background between the hangars is the Miles Falcon Six, the Vickers communications aircraft, in which Jeffrey Quill, Summers' Assistant Experimental Test Pilot, had flown him from Martlesham Heath in Suffolk for the maiden flight.

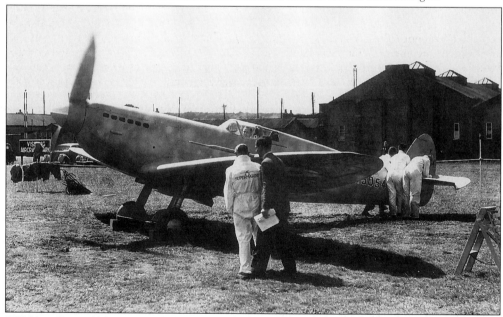

K5054, still simply know as 'The Fighter' and yet to be given its famous official name, in 'works finish' (ie. unpainted except for primer) seen here with its engine running and its special two-bladed fine-pitch propeller immediately before its first flight. Ken Scales, Flight Foreman in Charge, (in overalls and who later became Area Manager of the Reading wartime Spitfire production dispersal unit) is accompanied by Trevor Westbrook, Production Manager.

Immediately after the first flight of the prototype Spitfire K5054. Left to right: 'Mutt' Summers, Vickers Chief Test Pilot; Major H.J. Payn, R.J. Mitchell's Technical Assistant; Reginald Mitchell, Vickers-Supermarine Chief Designer; Stuart Scott-Hall, Air Ministry Resident Technical Officer (RTO) at Supermarine; Jeffrey Quill, who had recently joined Summers from the Royal Air Force as Assistant Experimental Test Pilot and who took over from him shortly after the first flight to lead the Supermarine flight test team throughout the ten-year Spitfire development programme. Summers had joined Vickers Aviation Ltd. at Weybridge from the Aeroplane and Armament Experimental Establishment (A&AEE) at Martlesham Heath in Suffolk in 1928, the same year that Vickers took over Supermarine. Hence his responsiblities embraced the test flying of both components of the Company's aviation activities.

Summers showing off K5054 to the press cameras about a month after the first flight, the aircraft now painted in cerulean-blue finish.

Jeffrey Quill in K5054, which he flew for the first time on 26 March 1936, three weeks after the maiden flight and now fitted with undercarriage leg cover fairings.

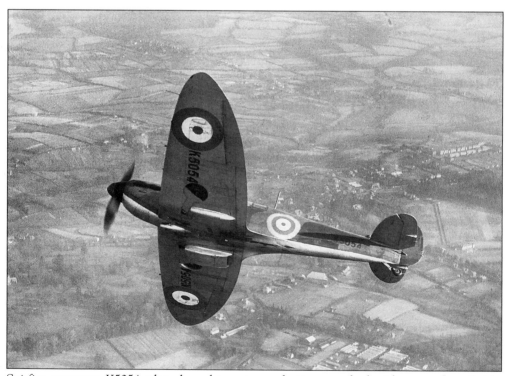

Spitfire prototype K5054 when brought up to production standard with camouflage finish, clearly demonstrating the distinctive elliptical wing planform.

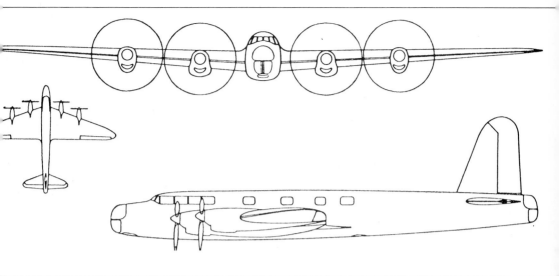

Reginald Mitchell's last design – the Vickers-Supermarine Type 317 B.12/36 four-engined, long-range, heavy bomber of 1936 – which he envisaged would partner the Spitfire at the forefront of the Royal Air Force in countering the major conflict which he foresaw looming large once more in Europe.

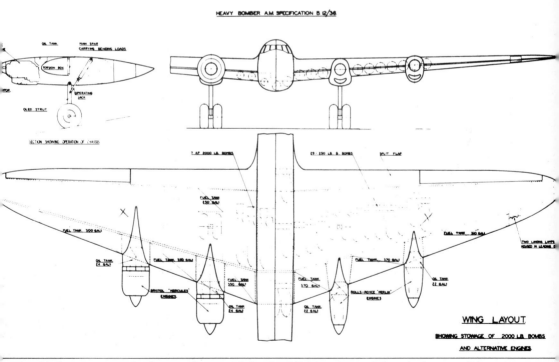

The 93 ft span swept-back wing layout of the B.12/36 bomber, of the single-spar, 'D'-nose torsion-box of the type developed by Supermarine over several years and used in the F.7/30 and the Spitfire, showing the stowage of seven 2,000 lb and twenty-nine 250 lb bombs, together with alternative engines (Rolls-Royce Merlin and Bristol Hercules).

A model of the Type 317 to heavy-bomber specification B.12/36.

One of the two Type 317 heavy-bomber prototype fuselages nearing completion at the Vickers-Supermarine factory at Itchen, shortly before they were destroyed by enemy action in September 1940.

Three

Winning the Schneider Trophy for Britain

When the internationally-prestigious Schneider Trophy was first awarded in 1913, the year Supermarine was founded, it was natural that a company dedicated to marine aircraft should take a keen interest in competing for it. Discontinued during the First World War, when the contest re-emerged in 1919, the Company persisted for the next twelve years under the inspired leadership of Reginald Mitchell to win the Trophy outright for Britain after the required three successive wins, also gaining three World Speed Records in the process.

Supermarine's first entry in 1919, its Sea Lion biplane commercial flying boat, was unsuccessful. But after the Italians had won the 1920 and 1921 contests, its Sea Lion II won the 1922 event, thus preventing Italy from taking the Trophy permanently.

After three specially-designed Curtiss seaplanes sponsored by the American Navy roundly beat Supermarine's Sea Lion III in 1923, Mitchell conceived his famous series of racing seaplanes, the S.4, which competed at Baltimore in 1925, the S.5 winning the Trophy at Venice in 1927, the S.6 winning over the Solent in 1929, and the S.6B winning it outright, again over the Solent, in 1931. This triumphant achievement was then of inestimable value in the conception of the Spitfire.

The Sea Lion I G-EALP being towed to the start of the 1919 Schneider Trophy race on 10 September at Bournemouth by the Supermarine launch Tiddleywinks to be flown by Sqn. Ldr. Basil D. Hobbs. The design of this aircraft was directed by F.J. Hargreaves, soon to be succeeded by Reginald Mitchell. Developed from the N.1B Baby and powered by a 450 hp Napier Lion pusher engine, this was the Company's first entry for the contest in the first year in which it was resumed after the First World War.

The 450 hp Napier Lion engine ready for installation in the Supermarine Sea Lion II for the 1922 Schneider Trophy event. In the background (left to right) are Hubert Scott-Paine (who took over the ownership and management of Supermarine from Pemberton-Billing in 1916), twenty-five year-old Reginald Mitchell and Wilf Elliott (who went on to became Works Superintendent for the whole of the Spitfire production dispersal operation across the South of England during the Second World War).

The Sea Lion II high-speed pusher flying-boat G-EBAH (before an extension to the top profile of the fin) on the River Itchen, Supermarine's triumphant British winner of the 1922 Schneider Trophy contest held at Naples. The 1920 contest had been won at Venice by the Italians with an uncontested fly-over by a Savoia S.19 flying-boat, and the 1921 race, again at Venice, with a fly-over in a Macchi M.7 flying-boat. However, the skill of Henri Biard, Supermarine's Chief Test Pilot, won the 1922 event to prevent the Italians taking the Trophy outright: Biard also won four World Records in the marine aircraft class.

The Supermarine Sea Lion III – the modified Sea Lion II with an increased-power 525 hp Napier Lion engine – the Company's unsuccessful entry in the 1923 Schneider Trophy event held at Cowes, Isle of Wight, with the Blackburn Pellet in the background.

Mitchell's radical and inspired Supermarine S.4 high-speed, wooden-construction, 680 hp Napier Lion-powered, racing seaplane entry for the 1925 Schneider Trophy contest under construction at the Woolston works.

The Supermarine S.4 being made ready at Calshot in August 1925 for that year's Schneider Trophy race, held on 23 October at Chesapeake Bay, Baltimore, USA. Flown by Henri Biard, Supermarine's Chief Test Pilot, it encountered wing flutter and was not successful. (The allocated serial number N197 was never worn).

A proud and happy Reginald Mitchell (centre) and his Supermarine team at Woolston on the threshold of dramatic achievement with N220, the second of the three S.5 900 hp geared-drive, Napier Lion-powered, metal-construction, racing seaplanes designed and built by Supermarine with full Government backing for the British entry in the 1927 Schneider Trophy race at Venice.

The Supermarine S.5 N220 Schneider Trophy seaplane being made ready for the 1927 race at Venice in September 1927. Piloted by Flt. Lt. S.N. Webster of the newly-formed Royal Air Force High Speed Flight, it won at an average speed of 281.65 mph. The direct-drive S.5 N219, flown by Flt. Lt. O.E. Worsley, took second place at 273.01 mph.

The 1927 Schneider Trophy winning Supermarine S.5 N220 together with its pilot, Flt. Lt. S.N. Webster.

The Vickers-Supermarine S.6 1929 Schneider Trophy race entry N247, which won the contest in the hands of Flg. Off. H.R.D. Waghorn, on a special towing lighter prior to the race.

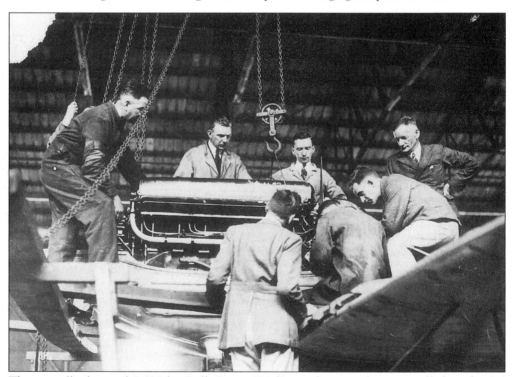

The specially-designed 2,530 hp Rolls-Royce 'R' (Racing) engine being installed in the S.6 racing seaplane.

Reginald Mitchell and Sir Henry Royce, two of Britain's greatest aeronautical engineers, in one of the industry's greatest-ever partnerships with their joint efforts in the Schneider Trophy contest which inspired a relationship between their two companies that was to endure for the next thirty-six years.

The sleek metal hull of the winning Vickers-Supermarine S.6 N247 seaplane closely cowling the big 2,350 hp direct-drive Rolls-Royce 'R' engine. Sqn. Ldr. Augustus Orlebar, Commander of the Royal Air Force High Speed Flight, also set a World Air Speed Record of 357.75 mph in this aircraft. Flt. Lt. Richard Atcherley established World Closed Circuit Air Speed Records over 50 km and 100 km at 332.49 and 331.75 mph respectively, in the second S.6 N248. All three records were set at Ryde, Isle of Wight, on 12 September 1929.

Reginald Mitchell and the Schneider Trophy S.6B team at Calshot: 1. L. Ransome (Aeronautical Inspection Directorate), 2. Major J. Buchanan (Air Ministry), 3. Flt. Lt G.H. Stainforth (Royal Air Force), 4. A.C. Lovesey (Rolls-Royce), 5. Sqn. Ldr. A.H. Orlebar (Royal Air Force), 6. W. Lappin (Rolls-Royce), 7. Reginald Mitchell, 8. Flt. Lt. H.R.D. Waghorn (Royal Air Force), Flg. Off. R.L.R. Atcherley (Royal Air Force).

The triumphant 1931 Schneider Trophy winning aircraft, the Vickers-Supermarine S.6B N1595, which was flown by Flt. Lt. John Boothman at Calshot on 13 September. Flt. Lt. George Stainforth also won a World Air Speed Record of 407.02 mph in this aircraft at Ryde, Isle of Wight, on the same day.

Dame Fanny Lucy Houston, the noted aeronautical philanthropist, who had inherited a large fortune from her late husband, a shipping magnate, and who generously donated £100,000 to sponsor Britain's entry in the 1931 Schneider Trophy contest in the absence of any support from the Ramsay Macdonald Government.

The 1931 Royal Air Force High Speed Flight Team (left to right): Flt. Lt. E.J. Linton Hope (a seaplane hull specialist), Lt. G.L. Brunton RN, Flt. Lts. F.W. Long and G. H. Stainforth, Sqn. Ldr. A.H. Orlebar, Flt. Lt. J.N. Boothman (winner), Flg. Off. L.G. Snaith, and Flt. Lt. Dry (engineer).

The Schneider Trophy. The triumphant Supermarine achievement for Britain. Reginald Mitchell's Supermarine team achieved four British victories in the Schneider Trophy contest series: In 1922 by Captain Henri Biard, Supermarine Chief Test Pilot, flying a Supermarine Sea Lion II at Naples achieving an average speed of 145.7 mph. In 1927 by Flight Lieutenant S.N. Webster of the Royal Air Force High Speed Flight flying the Supermarine S.5 N220 seaplane racer at Venice at an average speed of 281.65 mph. In 1929 by Flying Officer H.R.D. Waghorn flying the Supermarine S.6 N247 at Calshot, achieving a speed of 328.63 mph. In 1931 by Flight Lieutentant (later Air Chief Marshal Sir) John Boothman, also a member of the Royal Aero Club, flying the Vickers-Supermarine S.6B S1595, again at Calshot, at an average speed of 340.08 mph. Won outright for Great Britain by these last three consecutive victories, the strikingly impressive bronze trophy, displaying a sea nymph kissing a wave and encrusted with exotic sea creatures, became the absolute property of the Royal Aero Club in London where it resided for many years before being proudly exhibited in front of the ultimate winning Vickers-Supermarine S.6B at the Science Museum in London. The Trophy was appropriately displayed at Southampton in March 1996 during the celebrations of the sixtieth anniversary of the first flight of the Spitfire, to which it bequeathed such a notable heritage.

Four

The Nation-Saving
Spitfire

The unparalleled success of the Vickers-Supermarine Spitfire stemmed from its brilliant conception by Reginald Mitchell, continuing through a full decade of development – thanks to Joe Smith and Jeffrey Quill who continued to lead Mitchell's design and flying teams – through thirty-three different versions. With more than a doubling of engine power by Rolls-Royce with its Merlin and Griffon engines, these ranged from the two-and-a-half tons and the top speed of 362 mph of the Mk1 to the ultimate five-ton, 452 mph Seafire 47. A total of 22,749 Spitfires and Seafires were ultimately built in widely-dispersed production in Southern England and at the Government-owned shadow factory at Castle Bromwich in the Midlands.

Spitfire operational service spanned nineteen years, from the Mk1 joining Royal Air Force No. 19 Squadron at Duxford on 4 August 1938, in front-line combat service in all operational theatres throughout the Second World War, most notably the nation-saving role in the Battle of Britain in 1940, remaining in RAF service until June 1957, through to its final operational assignment in Malaya in 1959.

In addition to the RAF, the Commonwealth Air Forces and the USAAF, the Spitfire served as first-line equipment with nineteen foreign air forces – surely a uniquely-distinctive aeronautical record.

Right: Joe Smith CBE, MIMechE, FRAeS, 1898–1956. Worthy successor to Reginald Mitchell as Vickers-Supermarine's Chief Designer and responsible for the entire technical development of the Spitfire/Seafire genus from Mitchell's brilliant original conception, Joe Smith continued to lead his famous team into the early post-war years and the inauguration of age of jet fighters. Left: Jeffrey Kindersley Quill OBE, AFC, FRAeS, 1913–1996. Spitfire Test Pilot extraordinaire, responsible for the flight development of every Mark of Spitfire and Seafire throughout the entire decade-long development programme, Jeffrey Quill is seen here with Spitfire MK.VB AB910, appropriately registered QJ-J, of which he was the principal Vickers pilot in demonstrations at air shows in the post-war years until his last Spitfire flight in 1966, just thirty years after his first in the prototype K5054 in March 1936.

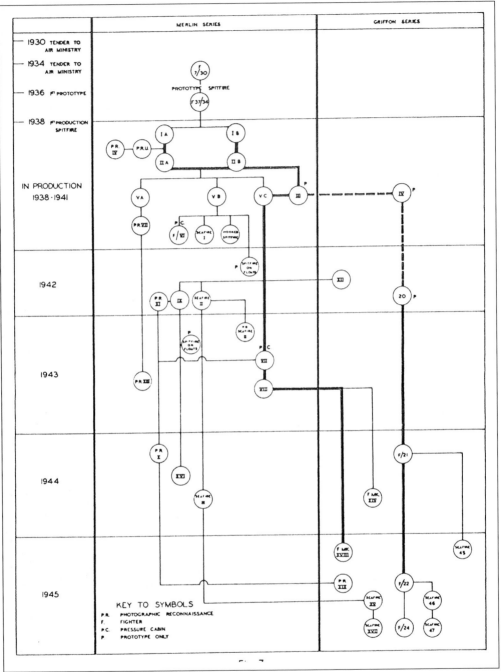

Spitfire/Seafire Genealogy. The evolution of the principal variants in the ten-year development pattern of the Spitfire/Seafire family to put into context the necessarily abbreviated, and somewhat arbitrary range of archive photographs of is what must, correspondingly, have been one of the most photographed aircraft types in aviation history.

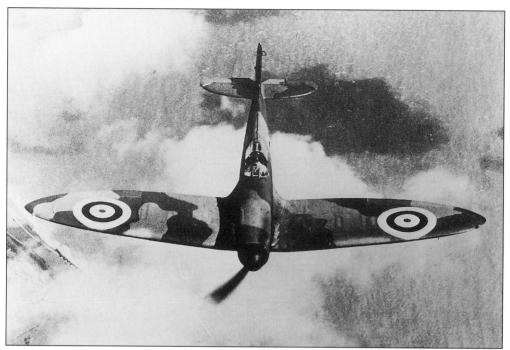

Spitfire Mk.1 with a de Havilland two-pitch propeller and painted in the standard RAF day-fighter camouflage scheme of Dark Earth and Green, as originally applied to the prototype K5054 when it was brought up to MK.1 standard.

The Speed Spitfire N.17 built in 1938 by the conversion of the forty-eighth production Spitfire Mk.I airframe and fitted with a specially-boosted 'Schneiderised Merlin' engine to provide maximum possible performance at low altitude for an attempt on the World Air Speed Record. However, when the Germans raised the record to 470 mph, the attempt was shelved. Nevertheless, the aircraft attacted much attention at the International Air Exhibition in Brussels in July 1939 and the whole episode did much to convince Joe Smith of the evident development potential of the Spitfire/Merlin combination.

Initial Spitfire Mk.Is lined up for inspection at Duxford, Cambridgeshire, the first Spitfire operational station and where the first Spitfire Mk.I joined Royal Air Force No. 19 Squadron on 4 August 1938.

Parade of Spitfire Mk.Is at Hornchurch, Essex, on 8 June 1939. K9910 heads the right hand section, K9912 the left. The cards hung under the aircraft read: 'Serviceable Aircraft'. K9910 was destroyed in the Battle of Britain (No. 65 Squadron) on 9 September 1940 and K9912 was used as a test-bed aircraft for the Merlin III engine.

HRH King George VI (left) being shown the cockpit of a Spitfire Mk.II at an unidentified Royal Air Force Station in November 1939.

Spitfire Mk.VBs of No. 485 (NZ) Squadron, formed at Driffield, Yorkshire, in March 1941. This squadron of Spitfires was subscribed for by the people of New Zealand and operated by the Royal New Zealand Air Force (RNZAF) with Royal Air Force Fighter Command from Kenley, Surrey.

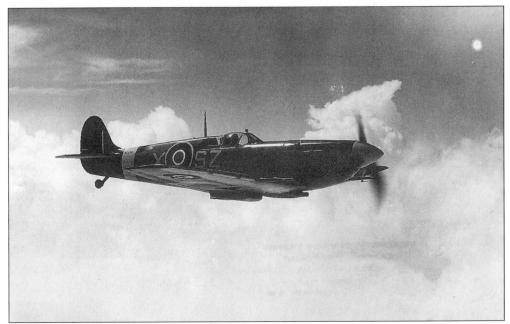

Spitfire Mk.VB of No. 316 (Polish) Squadron, based at Northolt, in early 1942.

British (Royal Air Force and Fleet Air Arm), American, Canadian, Polish and South American Spitfire pilots attending the newly-named Empire Central Flying School 'to try out new ideas and to gather fresh knowledge by experiment, which they will impart to the various training schools throughout the Empire'.

Pilots of the United States Army Air Force (USAAF) 4th Fighter Group, VIIIth Fighter Command with Spitfire Mk.Vs, putting on a 'scramble' for the benefit of press cameras at Debden, Essex in 1942.

Another American/Spitfire connection: Spitfire Mk.IX N74138 of the Embassy of the United States of America Civil Air Attaché, London.

Spitfire Mk.IXs of Royal Air Force No. 611 Squadron in early 1943 at the famous 1940 Battle of Britain Spitfire station, Biggin Hill, Kent.

Spitfire Mk.IX in Soviet Air Force markings. On 4 October 1942, the Soviet Ambassador in London presented a request for the urgent delivery of Spitfires to relieve the critical pressure on the Stalingrad front. With the approval of Winston Churchill, 137 Spitfire Mk.VBs drawn from Middle East stocks, plus 50 in spares, were handed over to the Russians early in 1943 at Basrah in Iraq. Of the total 1,332 Spitfires eventually delivered to Russia, 1,188 were Mk.IXs and all but a handful of PR Mk.IXs and Mk.XIs arrived via Iraq.

Two attempts were made to convert Spitfires for water-borne missions. The first was with a Spitfire Mk.I for operation from sheltered waters during the Norwegian campaign but this was abandoned because of the early termination of the campaign. The second attempt involved three such conversions by Folland Aircraft at Hamble, Hampshire. Shipped to Egypt onboard the SS *Penrith Castle* in October 1943, training was undertaken on the Great Bitter Lake. These aircraft were intended to become part of a complex air/sea mission supplied by Royal Navy submarines to attack German Junkers Ju52 tri-motor transports flying between Greece and Crete on refuelling missions. However, the conversion was not operationally successful and the whole daring plan was never implemented, being abandoned in 1943 when German forces occupied the Dodecanese islands.

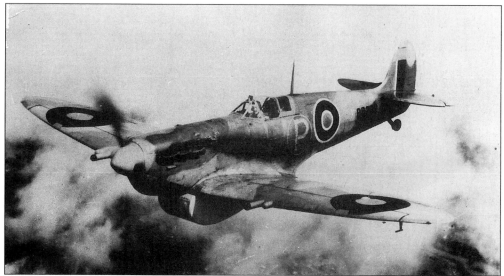

Spitfire Mk.VC with a 170-gallon ferry fuel tank, one of the few external excrescences detracting substantially from the classic, aesthetically-pleasing and aerodynamically-efficient Spitfire shape. However, this tank was not used operationally, but only for ferry purposes. Some Spitfire Mk.IXs were used operationally with a 30-gallon slipper tank and some Mk.VBs with a 90-gallon slipper tank. More than 300,000 Spitfire drop tanks were manufactured.

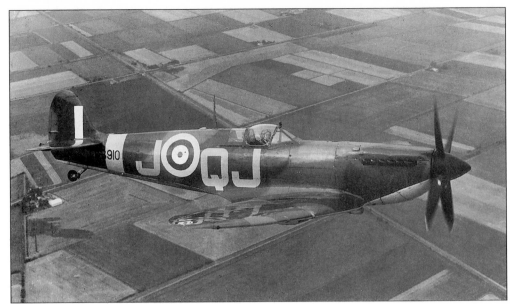

One of the best known of all Spitfires, the Mk.VB AB910. Built at Castle Bromwich in August 1941, it saw service with South African, Indian, American and Canadian squadrons. When at No. 53 Operational Training Unit (OTU) at Hibaldstow, Lincolnshire, the unauthorised passenger flight of Leading Aircraftswoman Margaret Horton took place when she was still hanging on to the tail when this aircraft took off after engine running, and completed a circuit in the air with her lying across the tail. Passing onto the civil register after the war, AB910 was returned to Vickers who operated it for many years until 1965 when the company's successors, British Aircraft Corporation (BAC), presented it to the RAF Battle of Britain Memorial Flight (BBMF). It continues to operate with the BBMF to this day, but now in the markings of AE-H 402 Squadron, which it carried when flying over the Normandy beaches on 6 June 1944.

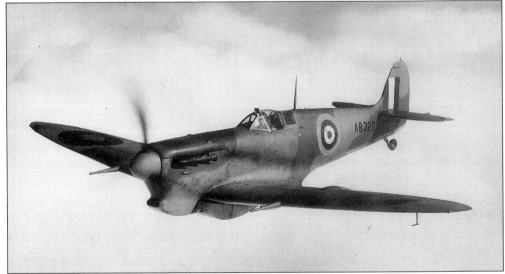

Spitfire Mk.VB AB320 tropicalised for use in the Middle East operations in the Western Desert and incorporating a special air intake duct under the nose fuselage housing a Vokes Millivee sand filter.

Turkish Spitfire Mk.VB formating with a German Focke-Wulf Fw190A-5. The two types operated side-by-side until they were replaced by North American P47D Thunderbolts in the late 1940s. Turkey took delivery of 56 Spitfire Mk.VBs and 185 Mk.IXs from 1943 onwards.

The Rolls-Royce Merlin 64 engine installation in a Spitfire Mk.VII.

Photo-reconnaissance (PR) Spitfire Mk.XI powered by a Rolls-Royce Merlin 63 engine and carrying US Army Air Force (USAAF) insignia, the last model having the Merlin engine.

Spitfire MK.VII prototype AB450, a converted Mk.V, with 'pointed' wing-tips for high-altitude operation.

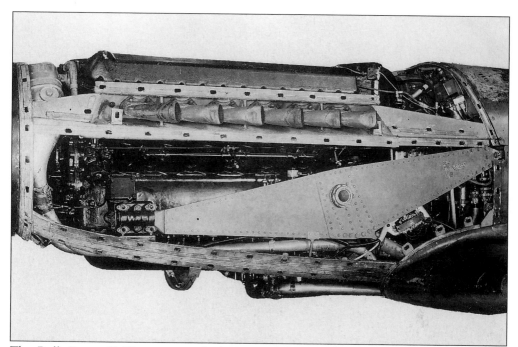

The Rolls-Royce Griffon engine which superseded the Merlin in later Marks of Spitfire. Basically 23 per cent larger in capacity than the Merlin, with a stronger fabricated mounting replacing the Merlin's tubular design, the Griffon eventually took the power output to 2,350 hp, compared to the 1,000 hp of the initial Merlin and the ultimate 1,500 hp Merlin 64.

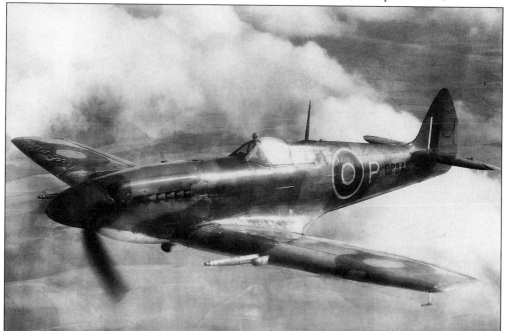

Spitfire Mk.IV/Mk.XII DP 845, the first Rolls-Royce Griffon-powered Spitfire and the 'favourite aeroplane' of Jeffrey Quill, the renowned Vickers-Supermarine Chief Test Pilot. One of two such prototypes, it was progressively fitted with Griffon IIB, IV and VI engines.

JF316, the first of four Spitfire Mk.VIII test bed aircraft conversions with the Rolls-Royce Griffon 61 engine as Spitfire Mk.XIV prototypes.

Rolls-Royce Griffon-powered Spitfire MK.XII with 'clipped' wings, pointed tail and fairings on the engine cowlings.

Spitfire Mk.IX, one of the first RAF Spitfires to fly alone into Germany, about to take-off on 26 March 1944. These aircraft flew over enemy territory between Aix-la-Chapelle and Cologne, shooting up German fighters and gliders, railway wagons and locomotives, and returning without loss after a sortie of about 800 miles.

Spitfire Mk.IXE MJ329 en-route to Normandy soon after the D-Day landings in June 1944. On gaining air superiority, Spitfires were operating in France for the first time since 1940 – on D-Day plus one. The intruder bomb racks on this aircraft were used for unconventional missions carrying two eighteen-gallon barrels of beer to the troops, a typical propaganda effort of the period. The design work for accommodating the barrels was performed as 'installation of Mk.XXX depth charge'. A second aircraft carried the beer in a long-range tank.

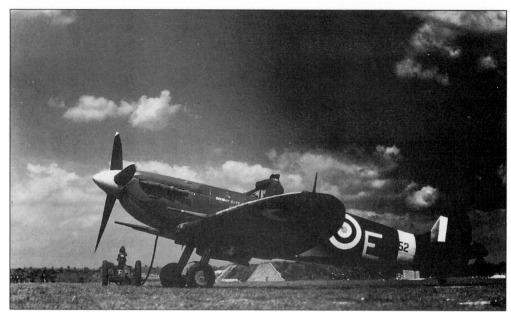

Spitfire Mk.VB being made ready for one of the many fighter formation sweeps deep into enemy-occupied France throughout daylight hours. By forcing the German Luftwaffe to deploy more than fifty per cent of its fighting strength in Western Europe, Royal Air Force offensive sweeps also aided Soviet forces on the Eastern front. Bomb-carrying and cannon-firing Spitfires made effective low-level attacks on German airfields, barracks, shipping, gun-positions, communications centres and, for specific targets, escorting bombers.

Spitfire Mk.24 flanked by a Mk.21 and a Mk.22.

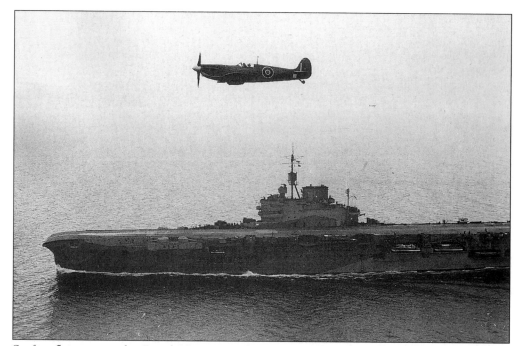

Seafire flying over the Royal Navy aircraft carrier HMS *Indomitable*. Altogether, Seafires operated with twenty-five front-line Royal Navy service squadrons and were based on twenty-five carriers. They also served with eighteen, second-line, naval service squadrons and three reserve squadrons.

Cannon-armed Seafire Mk.I embarked on the Royal Navy aircraft carrier HMS *Victorious* in 1942.

Seafire Mk.Is lined up for take-off on board HMS *Indefatigable*.

Seafire Mk.III with wings folded for on-board hangar stowage.

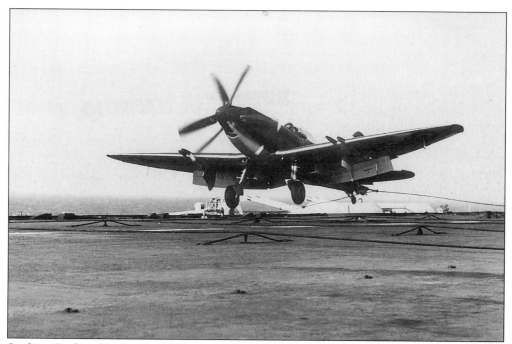

Seafire 47, the ultimate development of the Spitfire genus and which corresponded to the RAF's Spitfire Mk.24. Seafire 47s from the carrier HMS *Triumph* took part in operations in Korea in 1950.

Seafires arriving at St Peter Port, Guernsey, with the Royal Naval Volunteer Reserve (RNVR) in September 1950.

Spitfire Mk.VIII MT818 converted in 1946 as a two-seat trainer with Class B marking N32. The front cockpit was moved forward to accommodate the pupil and a raised rear cockpit was provided for the instructor. Around thirty Spitfire MK.IXs were converted for overseas sales as T8 and T9 trainers.

After being used extensively for overseas demonstrations, the Spitfire N32 two-seat trainer conversion subsequently became a private aircraft with the civil registration G-AIDN and named *Reginald Mitchell*.

Indian Air Force Spitfire T.Mk.IX HS534 two-seat trainer.

Three Spitfire Mk.IX two-seat trainers for the Royal Netherlands Air Force (RNAF) awaiting delivery to Valkenburg from the Vickers-Supermarine assembly plant and airfield at Eastleigh, Southampton.

Spitfire LF Mk.XVIE TE439 of No. 604 Squadron Royal Air Force Reserve Command at Hendon in August 1948.

Spitfire F.Mk.XII of No. 608 Squadron Royal Air Force at Thornaby, Yorkshire, in 1948.

Spitfire F.Mk.21 of the Royal Egyptian Air Force, one of a batch of twenty supplied in 1950. Egypt had earlier received thirty-seven Spitfire Mk.IXs between August and September 1946, some of which saw combat in the Arab-Israeli war of 1948-49, the only conflict in which Spitfire fought Spitfire.

Converted Seafire Mk.XV UB403 (formerly SR642) of the Union of Burma Air Force and originally built by Westland. In 1951, Burma took delivery of twenty de-navalised Seafire Mk.XVs, refurbished by Airwork Ltd. at Gatwick.

Spitfire Mk.XIX PM631, the last operational Spitfire at Royal Air Force Biggin Hill, Kent, in September 1957.

Spitfires and Hurricanes of the Battle of Britain Memorial Flight being led by the well-known Spitfire MK.VB AB910/QJ-J, Jeffrey Quill's post-war air show mount.

Five

War and Pieces

Hitherto a small organisation building specialised 'one-offs' or only small production runs, when the initial order for 310 Spitfires came in June 1936, only two months after the first flight of the prototype, the advanced nature of the all-metal design meant that a whole new production concept was required. Accordingly, with the outbreak of the Second World War in 1939 and the Woolston and Itchen factories already working at full output in conjunction with numerous subcontractors, a suitable dispersal scheme had also been instituted in the Southampton area.

The complete dispersal of Spitfire production into five centres across the South of England, with sixty-five units supplying piece parts, following the devastating bombing of the two parent factories in September 1940, ultimately realised more than 8,500 aircraft. The Spitfire was the only Allied aircraft programme in continuous development, production and active service throughout the war, with a total of 22,749 Spitfires and Seafires being built.

The huge Government-owned shadow factory at Castle Bromwich, near Birmingham, was responsible for more than half and Cunliffe-Owen, alongside Supermarine at Eastleigh Airport, and Westland at Yeovil, also produced large numbers. Meanwhile, more than 1,000 Supermarine Walrus and Sea Otter air/sea rescue amphibians were built by the other Solent area seaplane specialist, Saunders-Roe.

While it was becoming increasingly clear that the Spitfire and Walrus would be the primary Vickers-Supermarine types that would be required in large numbers in the impending conflict in Europe, the Company did respond to the Air Ministry requirement S.24/37 issued in November 1937 for a shipborne torpedo dive-bomber reconnaissance aircraft to replace the Fairey Albacore. The result was the Type 322 Dumbo. However, because of the growing preoccupation with the production and development of the Spitfire, the in-flight variable incidence wing design (the world's first) took longer to realise than the winning Fairey Barracuda and only two prototypes were built.

The Rolls-Royce Merlin-powered Vickers-Supermarine Dumbo aircraft with the fully-slotted and extensively-flapped, small-area wings, tightly-folded for carrier-borne use and visibly explaining its nickname because of the elephantine appearance. A large wing incidence setting at low speeds enabled the high lift system to be deployed to full advantage while still affording a reasonable fuselage attitude and normal airflow over the tail. The adjustable correlation of the wing and fuselage incidence also promoted aerodynamic efficiency at cruising and higher speeds, gave the pilot a better view of the deck in 'three-point' landings, and enabled the nose to be depressed on the approach or when sighting for dive-bombing.

Spitfire wing assembly at the Vickers-Supermarine works at Woolston in 1939.

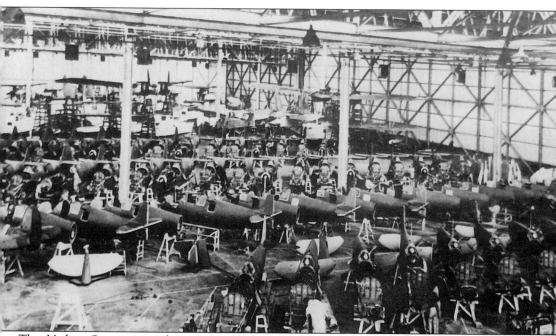

The Vickers-Supermarine factory at Itchen in 1939 with large-scale assembly of Spitfire fuselages fronting final assembly of the Stranraer and Walrus. This additional factory had been constructed a year earlier on land reclaimed from the River Itchen as a sister unit upstream from the parent factory at Woolston and was originally intended for the quantity production of the Walrus amphibian.

Spitfire final assembly by Vickers-Supermarine at Eastleigh Aerodrome (now Southampton Airport) in 1939 which continued there throughout the Second World War, and where Seafires were later also built by Cunliffe-Owen.

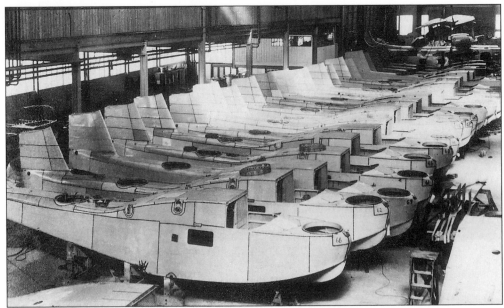

Early production of Vickers-Supermarine Walrus I hulls at the Itchen works prior to the bombing in 1940.

The main Vickers-Supermarine works at Woolston, after its complete destruction by the German Luftwaffe in September 1940 which resulted in the immediate massive dispersal of Spitfire production to five centres across the South of England. Two Spitfire Mk.Is built at Woolston in 1939 were bought by the City of Southampton to help the war effort and were registered and named R7059 *Southampton I* and R7060 *Southampton II* respectively. Their immediate predecessor was R7058 which was named in honour of the legendary Spitfire designer, Reginald J. Mitchell, written in script just below the pilot's canopy.

Squadron Commander Sir James Bird, who joined Supermarine in 1919 from the Royal Naval Air Service (RNAS) to fly Supermarine Channel flying boats between Southampton and the Isle of Wight and who took over the management of the company from Hubert Scott-Paine in 1923, before it was acquired by Vickers Limited in 1928, when he was appointed to the Board of Directors until 1937. He returned in 1940 to become General Manager of the entire South of England Spitfire production dispersal operation during the Second World War and was knighted in 1945.

The Vickers-Supermarine administrative headquarters, commercial and design offices at Hursley Park, near Winchester from 1940 to 1957, hitherto the home of Lady Cooper, wife of Sir George Cooper of Strong Breweries. Since it was vacated by Vickers-Supermarine in 1957, this impressive edifice has been operated as the IBM UK Laboratories.

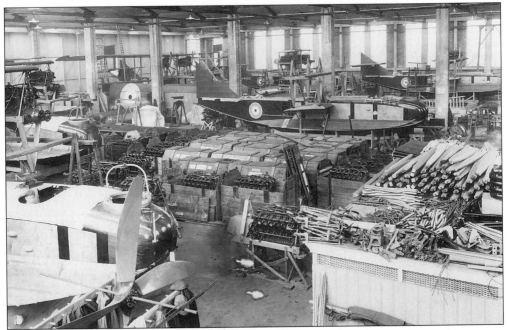

Production of the Walrus amphibian by Saunders-Roe, the pioneering marine aircraft company at West Cowes, Isle of Wight, to which the lion's share of production of the Walrus/Sea Otter family was subcontracted during the Second World War, enabling Vickers-Supermarine to concentrate exclusively on the Spitfire.

Production of Spitfire fuselages on the top floor of Seward's motor garage in Southampton, one of the twenty-eight dispersal units in the Southampton area requisitioned after the bombing of the Woolston and Itchen factories and which together employed a total of 3,000 people.

Spitfire fuselage assembly at the Wessex Motors garage dispersal unit at Salisbury, Wiltshire.

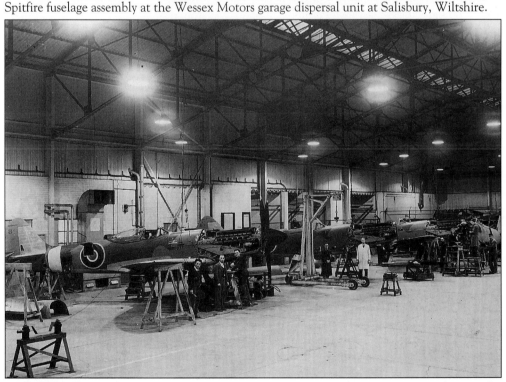

Assembly and flight test of Spitfire F.Mk.XVIIIs at Keevil aerodrome serving the Spitfire production unit at Trowbridge, Wiltshire.

The huge Government-owned shadow factory at Castle Bromwich, near Birmingham, where more than half the total of 22,749 Spitfires and Seafires were built and which was managed by Vickers-Armstrongs, the parent company of Vickers-Supermarine. Castle Bromwich also had its own satellite support units which included South Marston, near Swindon, (formerly Phillips and Powis), Cosford, Desford, a carpet factory at Kidderminster, an old prison at Worcester, silk stocking and celluloid doll factories at Leicester, the Midland Bus garage at Shrewsbury, an old iron foundry at Wellington, and Dudley Zoo.

Large-scale production of Spitfire fuselages at Castle Bromwich.

Mass-produced Spitfires awaiting flight testing and delivery at the Government-owned shadow factory at Castle Bromwich, with Avro Lancaster bombers which were also produced there.

Spitfire Mk.IIA P8329, one of the first 1,000 aircraft built at Castle Bromwich and named *Sumbawa* after an island in the Indonesian archipelago.

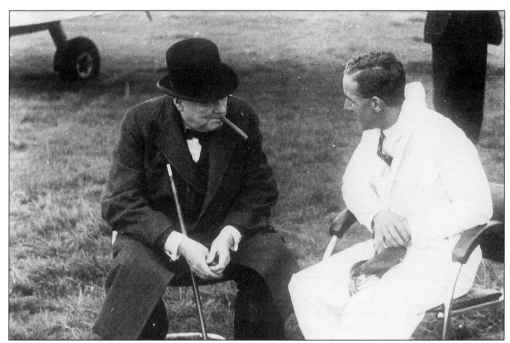

Alex Henshaw MBE, the brilliant Vickers Chief Test Pilot at Castle Bromwich throughout the Second World War, in discussion with Britain's famous war leader, Winston Churchill, after demonstrating a Spitfire Mk.V there in 1942. Between June 1940 and January 1946, 11,694 Spitfires and 305 Lancasters were produced at Castle Bromwich and the dispersal factories at Cosford and Desford. During these five-and-a-half years of test flying, Alex Henshaw and his team of twenty-five, short-stay, mainly service pilots, flew 8,210 hours on Spitfire production and perfomance trials, and 344 hours on Lancasters, involving 33,918 Spitfire test flights and 900 for Lancasters.

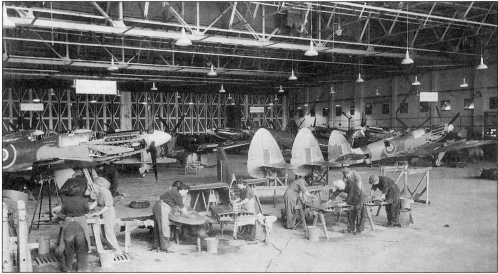

Production of Rolls-Royce Griffon-powered Spitfire MK.21s and 24s at South Marston, near Swindon, Wiltshire, which site was initially a satellite of Castle Bromwich and became the ultimate headquarters of Vickers-Supermarine in 1958.

Spitfire Production

Mark	Number built	Organisation
Prototype	1	Vickers-Supermarine
I	1,530	Vickers-Supermarine
	50	Westland
IB	About 30	Vickers-Supermarine
IIA, IIB, IIC	920	Vickers-Armstrongs Castle Bromwich
III	2	Vickers-Supermarine
IV	1	Vickers-Supermarine
PR.IV	229	Vickers-Supermarine
VA	1,367	Vickers-Supermarine
VB	4,477	Vickers-Armstrongs Castle Bromwich
VC	636	Westland
VI	100	Vickers-Supermarine
VII	140	Vickers-Supermarine
PR.VII		Service modification of Mk.VA
VIII	1,650	Vickers-Supermarine
IX	561	Vickers-Supermarine
	5,104	Vickers-Armstrongs Castle Bromwich
PR.X	16	Vickers-Supermarine
PR.XI	471	Vickers-Supermarine
XII	100	Vickers-Supermarine
PR.XIII	18	Vickers-Supermarine
XIV	957	Vickers-Supermarine
XVI	1,054	Vickers-Armstrongs Castle Bromwich
XVIII	300	Vickers-Supermarine
PR.XIX	225	Vickers-Supermarine
XX	1	Vickers-Supermarine
XXI	122	Vickers-Armstrongs Castle Bromwich
XXII	16	Vickers-Supermarine
XXIV	54	Vickers-Armstrongs Castle Bromwich

In addition to the Royal Air Force, the Royal Navy, the Fleet Air Arm and the Commonwealth Air Forces of Australia, Canada, India, New Zealand, Rhodesia and South Africa, and the United States Army Air Force (in the Middle East with 600 aircraft on loan from the RAF), the Spitfire and Seafire family was operated by nineteen other airforces – Belgium, Burma, China, Czechoslovakia, Denmark, Egypt, Eire, France, Greece, Israel, Italy, Netherlands, Norway, Portugal, Siam, Sweden, Syria, Turkey and the USSR. Argentina is also believed to have operated a single aircraft.

Seafire
Production

Mark	Number built	Organisation
IB	About 170	Air Service Training
IIC	262	Vickers-Supermarine
	110	Westland
III	900	Westland
	350	Cunliffe-Owen
XV	6	Vickers-Supermarine
	250	Westland
XVII	212	Westland
	20	Cunliffe-Owen
45	50	Vickers-Armstrongs Castle Bromwich
46	24	Vickers-Supermarine
47	90	Vickers-Supermarine

"The Last of the Many".

delivered Dec. 1946.

Air Service Training (AST) at Hamble, near Portsmouth, played an important role in the Spitfire programme. In addition to the repair of 3,507 battle-damaged aircraft between 1940 and 1946, AST also built about 170 Seafires.

Six

Into the Jet Age and the Final Years

The exemplary step-by-step development of the Spitfire throughout the Second World War proved to be the inspirational model whereby Supermarine embraced the two major new technical innovations which characterised post-war combat aircraft – the jet engine and swept wings – and the realisation of three generations of jet fighters.

Marrying the 'laminar-flow' wings of the Spiteful/Seafang – the ultimate in Supermarine's piston-engined lineage – with the first-generation centrifugal jet engine, the Rolls-Royce Nene, resulted in the Attacker of 1944, which became the Royal Navy's first operational jet fighter. Then came the Swift, the first British swept-wing fighter to join the RAF, which also raised the World Air Speed record to 735.7 mph in Libya in 1953.

The ultimate Supermarine aircraft type, the big Scimitar naval fighter, entered service with the Royal Navy in 1958. The issue of the last Scimitar at the Vickers-Supermarine South Marston (Swindon) factory in 1963 marked the end of half a century of outstanding achievement from which Vickers-Armstrongs and the British Aircraft Corporation continued to benefit for many years thereafter. During these final years, Supermarine also engaged in pioneering work on Hovercraft and important original thinking for the BAC TSR2 supersonic fighter which directly prefaced the European Tornado of today.

The Vickers-Supermarine Type 371 Spiteful, the last of the Company's famous piston-engined fighter lineage, designed to Air Ministry Specification F.1/43 and Operational Requirement 120. With a new, high-speed, laminar-flow wing and four 20 mm cannon matched to a Spitfire F.Mk.XIV fuselage and a 2,375 hp Rolls-Royce Griffon 69 engine, it was a substantially new aircraft. N660, the first prototype, was first flown by Jeffrey Quill on 30 June 1944.

Production Spiteful RB520 with mock-up of the pilot's canopy for the Seafang, its naval counterpart. The first production Spiteful (NN664) was flown on 2 April 1945, a month before the end of the war in Europe. Only seventeen production aircraft were flown and there was no service use.

Seafang F.31 VG471, the first of only ten production aircraft of the 150 initially ordered to specification N.5/45. Ten F.32s were also built. However, although neither of the Spiteful/Seafang siblings were produced in quantity, they constituted an important contribution to transonic aerodynamics and their jet-powered successors.

Seafang F.Mk.32 powered by a 2,350 hp Rolls-Royce Griffon 87 engine with contra-rotating propellers in December 1946. While the Admiralty preferred to carry on with the Seafire, a further high-speed design powered by a Rolls-Royce Eagle 46H piston engine was drawn up in June 1944 as the Type 391 but was eventually dropped in favour of the Type 392 to Specification E.10/44, which became the Royal Navy's first jet fighter, the Attacker.

Reviving the name Seagull from its successful Schneider Trophy seaplanes of the 1920s, the last of the long line of Supermarine flying boats was the Seagull ASR.Mk.1 carrier-borne, air-sea rescue amphibian, designed to Specification S.12/40, with a Rolls-Royce Griffon engine and contra-rotating propellers. The first prototype PA143 was first flown on 14 July 1948 from the water at Itchen by Lt. Cdr. Mike Lithgow, who had joined Vickers-Supermarine from the Fleet Air Arm, and appeared at the SBAC Farnborough Air Show two months later.

PA147, the second prototype Seagull ASR.1 undergoing deck-landing trials. Intended to succeed the Walrus/Sea Otter, with advantage being taken of the variable-incidence wing concept of the Type 322 Dumbo, after an extensive four-year trials and experimental period, numerous modifications, and the gaining of a World Air Speed Record for amphibians at 241.9 mph when participating in the Air League Cup race on 22 July 1950, the programme was terminated in 1952.

TS409, the first prototype Vickers-Supermarine Attacker, the Royal Navy's first jet-powered aircraft type designed to Specification E.10/44 and directly developed from the moribund Spiteful. Marrying the high-speed laminar wing of the Spiteful with a rotund fuselage to accommodate the 5,000 lb thrust Rolls-Royce Nene turbojet, the first flight was made at Boscombe Down on 27 July 1946, by Jeffrey Quill.

Navalised Attacker WA493 onboard an aircraft carrier. One hundred and forty-nine Attackers were built for the Royal Navy. A further thirty-six were supplied to the Pakistan Air Force which were delivered to Karachi in June 1951 and May 1953. All Attackers were built at Hursley Park, transported to High Post for final assembly and first flown from Boscombe Down.

The Attacker FB.2 with overload fuel tank and one of many possible weapon-carrying configurations. Mike Lithgow, who succeeded Jeffrey Quill as the Vickers-Supermarine Chief Test Pilot, captured the International 100 km Closed Circuit Record at 564.88 mph on 27 February 1948 and won the SBAC Challenge Cup at 533 mph in July 1950 with T416, the third prototype Attacker. As a pioneering type, the Attacker played a vital role in the transition from the piston-engined, propeller-driven fighter to pure jet propulsion.

VV106, the first of two prototype Vickers-Supermarine Type 510 high-speed, single-seat, single-engined fighters designed to Air Ministry specification E.41/46, a developed version of the Attacker with 40-degree swept-back wings and intended to serve as a Gloster Meteor replacement. Built at Hursley Park, it was first flown by Mike Lithgow from Boscombe Down on 29 December 1948. This was the first British jet-engined aircraft to fly with sweepback on both the wing and horizontal tail surfaces.

VV119, the second prototype Swift, originally built as the Vickers-Supermarine Type 528 with a tailwheel undercarriage. VV106, the first prototype, first flown as the Type 510 by Mike Lithgow on 29 December 1948 from Boscombe Down, became the first swept-wing aicraft to land-on and take-off from an aircraft carrier, HMS *Illustrious*, and later became the Type 517 with a hinged empennage and variable-incidence tail. First flown on 27 March 1950, V119 was grounded two months later for conversion to a nosewheel layout and redesignated Type 535, before flying again on 23 August 1950.

VV119, the second prototype Swift, was named *Prometheus* in 1951 when it was used as the 'star' of the full-length public feature film *The Sound Barrier*. It was flown by Vickers-Supermarine test pilot, Dave Morgan, and others: a unique experience for a prototype aircraft still on test.

Swift F.4 WK198, which Mike Lithgow, Vickers-Supermarine's Chief Test Pilot, used for his attempt on the World Speed Record, at the test airfield at Chilbolton, Hampshire, on 22 September 1953, shortly before departure for North Africa.

Swift WK198 over Tripoli harbour during the World Air Speed record attempt in 1953. After displaying this aircraft at the 1953 SBAC Show at Farnborough, on 26 September 1953 – in the coronation year of HM Queen Elizabeth II and the fiftieth anniversary year of the birth of powered flight – Mike Lithgow set up a World Air Speed record of 735.7 mph at Castle Idris near Tripoli, in Libya. The normal maximum speed of the Swift F.Mk.IV with reheat was 709 mph at sea level.

The third production Swift F.Mk.I WK196 at the Vickers-Supermarine flight test and delivery preparation hangar at Chilbolton, Hampshire, together with the second prototype VV119 and the first two production aircraft, WK194 and WK195, in the background.

Swift F.2s at South Marston ready for delivery to No. 2 Squadron Tactical Air Force, based at Geilenkirchen, West Germany. The Swift was the RAF's first British swept-wing aircraft.

The prototype Swift F.Mk.VII XF113 fitted with Fairey Fireflash guided missiles.

WJ 960, the first pre-production Swift, accompanied by Spitfire F.MK.22 PK542. A total of 193 Swifts were built plus four prototypes.

The development Type 508/529 (VX133/VX136) designed to specification N.9/47, project predecessor of the definitive Scimitar single-seat, twin-engined, naval jet fighter, during aircraft carrier deck-landing trials. The 'butterfly' tail was used to promote the necessary strength in the fine thickness/chord ratio surfaces and to clear the twin Rolls-Royce Avon jet engine effluxes.

The Vickers-Supermarine Type 508 and Swift, airborne together.

The Vickers-Supermarine Type 544 WT859, the third of the three Scimitar production prototypes ordered to Specification N.113D, during steam-catapult proving trials on board the Royal Navy's premier aircraft carrier HMS *Ark Royal* in January 1957.

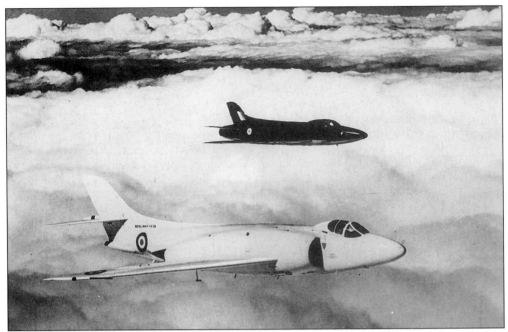

Symmetry in black and white – the Swift, the first British swept-wing aircraft to be operated by the Royal Air Force and the Scimitar, the Royal Navy's first swept-wing jet aircraft.

The definitive Vickers-Supermarine Scimitar F.1 naval strike fighter powered by two 10,000 lb. thrust Rolls-Royce Avon axial-flow turbojet engines and incorporating the advanced feature of 'flap-blowing' to improve lift, particularly for operation from aircraft carriers. This is XD212, the first production aircraft.

The Scimitar tightly-fitted with wings folded in the 25-ft diameter Stratosphere Chamber at Vickers-Armstrongs (Aircraft) Weybridge, Surrey. Designed by Barnes Wallis, built by Vickers (Shipbuilders) at Barrow-in-Furness, Cumbria, and commissioned in 1948, this unique low-temperature and high-altitude climatic test facility enabled the 'winterisation' trials of the Scimitar to be simulated, including engine runs (outside the chamber) after cold soak, and verified in the UK rather than in natural conditions in Canada or elsewhere in the Arctic region.

Line-up of Scimitars of Royal Navy No. 807 Squadron in their dispersal at the shore base at Lossiemouth, Scotland, prior to embarking in their 'home base', the aircraft carrier HMS Ark Royal – the 'R' on the aircraft tails indicating Ark Royal's 'ownership' of these aircraft.

125

The last of the eighty-two Vickers-Supermarine Scimitar naval fighters aircraft that were ultimately built, all at South Marston near Swindon (from where the last aircraft issued in 1963), awaiting delivery to the Royal Navy after final flight testing at the Vickers-Armstrongs (Aircraft) flight test centre at Wisley, Surrey, fifty years after the issue of Noel Pemberton-Billing's first 'Supermarine' at Southampton in 1913.

The Vickers Hovercraft VA.1 – with the aircraft-type 'Class B' registration G-15-252 – during trials on Southampton Water in October 1961. This was the first of a series of Hovercraft also developed in the final years of the Supermarine team and a classic example of the much-vaunted 'spin-off' from aviation experience – but under the aegis of Vickers-Armstrongs (Engineers) into which the non-aircraft elements of the Vickers-Supermarine team were absorbed after the transfer from Hursley Park, Hampshire, to South Marston, near Swindon, Wiltshire in 1957.

The Vickers Hovercraft VA.2-001 named *Southern Cross*. Employing the ground-effect air-cushion principle, it was completely free from surface contact and therefore truly amphibious. Vickers claims for this revolutionary type of transport vehicle were: '(Hovercraft) need no airfields, ports or prepared berthing facilities and, with a flexible speed range of 30 to 100 knots, fill the speed gap that exists between present forms of transport.'

The twin-engined VA-3 Hovercraft G-15-253 – first 'flown' on 25 April 1962 – in operation with British United Airways. Powered by two Bristol-Siddeley Turmo 603 gas-turbine engines, VA-3 had an all-up weight of 28,000 lb, carried 24 passengers and crew at a cruising speed of 70 mph with a surface clearance – hover height – of 8 in and operated the world's first commercial Hovercraft service between Wallasey and Rhyl in North Wales on 20 July 1962. As the Company's final expression of its brilliant record and experience in aeronautical technology, this could still be regarded as fittingly in the tradition of the original founding objective and definition of 'Supermarine', five decades earlier.

Acknowledgements

The privilege of knowing and working with many 'Supermariners', notably including some of Reginald Mitchell's original design team in their latter years, leads me to acknowledge first my profound gratitude to them, and many others like them, for the magnificent story which they created for me to retell pictorially here.

Because much valuable Supermarine archive material was unfortunately destroyed in a fire at Swindon in 1960, to do so has required the much-appreciated help of several good friends in providing appropriate pictures, information and support – and to whom I am correspondingly grateful for preserving this precious material in the first place.

In this respect, I especially wish to thank Peter Boxer, Brian Wexham and Dr Mark Nicholls for access to the Vickers PLC photographic archives now carefully preserved at the Cambridge University Library; to Gerry Gingell, for many years Supermarine's Head of Technical Publications and Exhibitions, for access to his extensive personal memorabilia; to Phil Jarrett, whose knowledge and photographic collection of early British aviation is unsurpassed; to Gordon Eldridge, Alan Jones and Don Upward of the R.J. Mitchell Memorial Museum at the Southampton Hall of Aviation; and to Eric Morgan who, with the late Charles Andrews, saved so much Supermarine archive material for posterity and publication for later generations.

I must also record my gratitude to Mike Hooks for originally suggesting that I should deal with both components of the Vickers aviation interests – Supermarine and Weybridge – in this commendable series.

Dr Norman Barfield
Weybridge
Surrey
August 1996